Reading Welsh

Reading Welsh
An Essential Companion

**D. Geraint Lewis
& Nudd Lewis**

Common Welsh words
in all their various forms
(mutated, inflected, infixed, etc.)

Gomer

Cyhoeddwyd yn 2014 gan Wasg Gomer, Llandysul, Ceredigion SA44 4JL
Published in 2014 by Gomer Press, Llandysul, Ceredigion SA44 4JL

ISBN 978-1-84851-870-4

Dymuna'r cyhoeddwyr gydnabod cymorth Cyngor Llyfrau Cymru.
The publishers wish to acknowledge the financial support
of the Welsh Books Council.

Argraffwyd a rhwymwyd yng Nghymru gan Wasg Gomer, Llandysul, Ceredigion
Printed and bound in Wales at Gomer Press, Llandysul Ceredigion

foreword & acknowledgements

This is a comprehensive listing, in their various forms, of the 10,000 most frequently used words in written Welsh. This is an invaluable tool for those new to reading Welsh, as many of these forms would not normally appear in a traditional Welsh dictionary. The companion also provides some basic initial guidelines on how to follow and understand text for readers new to the Welsh language.

The companion includes:

- mutated forms
- plural forms
- feminine forms
- the most frequently used verb forms
- personal forms of prepositions
- contracted and fixed forms.

A further innovation is that it sets out these words in English alphabetical order for those not familiar with the Welsh alphabetical order.

To include all the possible forms that exist for even a limited Welsh vocabulary would result in a tediously long list containing very many word-forms rarely used.

The present list draws on those words most frequently used in written Welsh and has been made possible by the work of Professor Kevin P. Scannell of the University of Saint Louis, Missouri, who has compiled a large corpus of Welsh words by electronically combing through a huge range of Welsh texts. Details of Professor Scannell's work may be found at http://borel.slu.edu/nlp.html.

We are extremely grateful to Professor Scannell for permission to draw on this work and also to Andrew Hawke, editor of the great University of Wales Dictionary, for making available to us the 10,000 most frequently used forms to appear in Professor Scannell's corpus.

The companion is also supported by an internet-based electronic Welsh dictionary, *Y Gweiadur* (www.gweiadur.com), and that dictionary is the result of bringing together these two electronic lexical sources.

Gratitude is due to the Editorial and Design departments of the Welsh Books Council who have provided us with their professional assistance.

D. Geraint Lewis & Nudd Lewis
Llangwyryfon

introduction

The Welsh language differs in so many respects from English that it is almost impossible to use current dictionaries of Welsh without having some understanding of what these differences are. The aim of this innovative companion is to make Welsh-language text more accessible to Welsh learners and to those who need to read extracts of Welsh text from time to time.

This companion sets out the most commonly used Welsh words in all their (what can be) bewildering varieties. It has a number of unique features to assist those who are relatively new to reading Welsh text.

unique features:

• It follows the **English alphabet** (which differs significantly from the Welsh alphabet used in dictionaries of Welsh).

• The most obvious and potentially confusing change is the way in which the first letter of a word can vary due to **mutation**. For the first time, the most common words are presented here in their mutated forms.

• The use of verb forms is more complex in Welsh than English due to **inflexion**. The most common of these verbs are set down in both their regular and mutated forms.

• Many adjectives in Welsh have both feminine and plural forms, e.g. white has a masculine form 'gwyn' and a feminine form 'gwen' and 'coch,' the Welsh word for red, has a plural form 'cochion'.

• Plural nouns do not follow a regular pattern such as adding 's' (cat – cats, etc.) as in English.

• Many prepositions (like verbs) have personal inflected forms in Welsh. For example, the Welsh word for in is 'yn', but the first person singular form is 'ynof'.

None of these individual forms would normally be included in a traditional dictionary of Welsh.

general guidelines for readers new to Welsh:

The order of the words in a Welsh sentence does not follow the same pattern as in English. You will find the meaning of the individual words here, but will have to rearrange the order of the words to make sense of the sentence.

1. Sometimes the translation of individual words can produce what looks like a question in English, e.g. 'is John here'. This is due to the different word order in Welsh where it means 'John is here'. So, unless there is a question mark in the text, it would be as well to treat any seeming question as a direct statement.

2. For questions, look out for a tell-tale question mark.

3. Negative (not) statements are introduced by 'Ni' or 'Na', or include the word 'ddim' (not).

4. There is no impersonal 'it' in Welsh, so sometimes you will need to translate 'he' or 'she' as 'it'.

5. There is no 'a' as in a *dog* in Welsh. The stand-alone noun (name) 'ci' means a *dog*.

6. Adjectives which normally appear before a noun in English, e.g. 'the red door', follow the noun in Welsh: y (the) *drws* (door) *coch* (red).

7. Welsh numerals are followed by the singular form of the noun, e.g. 'tri dyn' which translates literally as 'three man'.

8. This listing does not include idioms (e.g. 'going *flat out*', where the meaning of the phrase cannot be understood from the meaning of the individual words).

inflected verb forms

These are forms like 'went' or 'gone' from *go*, 'sat' from *sit*, and '(I) *am*', '(you) *are*', '(he/she) *is*', from the verb *to be*. With the exception of the heavily used forms of *to be* these have largely disappeared in English, however they are more frequently used in Welsh, being particularly important in narrative sequences (i.e. telling of past events).

syntax or sentence order

Most European languages follow the pattern: **Subject** (*John*) **Verb** (*saw*) **Object** (*the dog*). However the equivalent pattern in Welsh is: **Verb** (*Gwelodd*) **Subject** (*John*) **Object** (*y ci*).

mutation

At first sight, Welsh mutations may seem a very unfamiliar concept to the novice Welsh reader. However, surprisingly, this phenomenon also takes place in English, for example when 'f' changes to 'v' and *wolf* becomes *wolves*, or when the English 'int' as in *international* becomes 'inn' in the transatlantic *innernational.* Due to the way Welsh has developed from the earlier Brythonic language, these changes occur at the beginning of words in Welsh.

mutated forms of words

A word printed in *italic print* means that the root form
of that word begins with a different letter:

a	is a mutation of	**g**
b	is a mutation of	**p**
ch	is a mutation of	**c**
d	is a mutation of	**t**
dd	is a mutation of	**d**
e	is a mutation of	**g**
f	is a mutation of	either **b** or **m**
g	is a mutation of	**c**
h	is a mutation of	any vowel (**a, e, i, o, u** ALSO **w** and **y**)
l	is a mutation of	either **ll** or **g**
m	is a mutation of	**b**
mh	is a mutation of	**p**
n	is a mutation of	**d**
ng	is a mutation of	**g**
ngh	is a mutation of	**c**
nh	is a mutation of	**t**
o	is a mutation of	**g**
ph	is a mutation of	**p**
r	is a mutation of	either **rh** or **g**
th	is a mutation of	**t**
w	is a mutation of	**g**
y	is a mutation of	**g**

If you wish to look up words (set down here in the
order of the English alphabet) in a traditional Welsh
dictionary, you need to be aware of the Welsh
alphabetical sequence:

a b c **ch** d **dd** e f **ff** g **ng** h i j l **ll** m n o p **ph** r **rh** s t **th** u w y

For information, the pairs of letters in bold actually signify a single letter/sound in the Welsh alphabet. More details and examples are included at the start of each letter in this companion.

The definitions listed in this companion are arranged in order of the English alphabet and {.} are used to draw attention to a word's usage rather than its direct meaning.

Before proceeding it is important to note that whilst this companion includes an extensive range of the most common forms of words, it is not exhaustive. Every word does not appear in all its manifestations. As you continue reading in Welsh, you may therefore occasionally discover a word which does not appear in this volume. However, the guidance given above should help you to determine the standard form of the word, and if it is one which has been mutated, or which has been varied in some other way.

A : a

a word starting with **a** printed in *italics* means that the root form
of that word begins with **g**, e.g. *adael* root **gadael**

a[1] a, A
a[2] and
   a'ch[1] and your
   a'i[1] and his/her/its
   a'm[1] and my
   a'n[1] and our
   a'r and the
   a'th[1] and your
   a'u[1] and their
a[3] {*introduces a question*}
a[4] that, which, who, whom
   a'ch[2] that {…} you
   a'i[2] {…} him/her/it
   a'm[2] that {…} me
   a'n[2] that {…} us
   a'th[2] that {…} you
   a'u[2] that {…} them
â[1] as, with
   â'ch as your, with your
   â'i as his/her/its, with his/her/its
   â'm as my, with my
   â'n as our, with our
   â'r[1] as the, with the
   â'th as your, with your
   â'u as their, with their
â[2] (he/she/it) goes, will go
   â'r[2] the {…} goes, will go
ab son of
abaty abbey
aber confluence, mouth of river

aberoedd confluences, river mouths
aberth sacrifice
aberthu to sacrifice
abl able, rich, strong
absennol absent
absenoldeb absence
absenoldebau absences
absoliwt absolute, complete
abwyd bait, lure
ac and
academaidd academic, scholarly
academi academy
academydd academic
academyddion academics
acen accent, diacritic
acenion accents
acennog accented
ach[1] lineage, pedigree
ach[2] ugh!
achau family tree
achlysur occasion
achlysurol occasional
achlysuron occasions
achos[1] case, cause
achos[2] because
achosi to cause
achosion cases, causes
achosir (is/will be) caused
achosodd (he/she/it) caused
achoswyd (was) caused

achrededig accredited
achrediad accreditation
achredu to accredit
achub to save, to rescue
achwyn to complain
achwynwyr complainants
achwynydd complainant, plaintiff
achwynyddion complainants
acrobat acrobat
act act
actio to act, to imitate
actor actor
actores actress
actorion actors
acw that, there, those
ad (you) leave!
adael to leave
adain fin, spoke, wing
adar birds
adawodd (he/she/it) left
adawyd (was) left
adborth feedback
ad-dâl repayment
ad-daliad repayment
ad-dalu to recompense, to repay
addas suitable, worthy
addasiad adaptation, modification
addasiadau modifications
addasrwydd suitability
addasu to adapt
addaswyd (was) adapted
addawodd (he/she/it) promised
addawol auspicious, promising
addewid promise
addewidion promises
addo to promise
addoli to adore, to worship

addoliad adoration, worship
ad-drefnu to reorganise,
    to reshuffle
addurn decoration, ornament
addurniadau ornaments
addurno to decorate
addysg education
addysgiadol educational
addysgir (is/will be) educated,
    taught
addysgol educational
addysgu to educate, to teach
addysgwr educationalist
addysgwyr educationalists
adeg time
adegau times
adeilad building
adeiladau buildings
adeiladodd (he/she/it) built
adeiladol constructive
adeiladu to build, to construct
adeiladwaith construction,
    structure
adeiladwr builder
adeiladwyd (was) built
adeiladwyr builders
adeiledd structure
adeileddau structures
adeiledig built-up
aden fin, spoke, wing
adennill to recapture, to regain
adenydd wings
aderyn bird
adfail ruin
adfeilion ruins
adfer¹ remedial
adfer² to recover, to restore

adferiad recovery
adferol restoring
adfywiad recovery, regeneration
adfywio to recover, to revive
adio to add
adlais echo
adleoli to relocate
adlewyrchiad reflection
adlewyrchir (is/will be) reflected
adlewyrchu to reflect
adloniant entertainment,
     recreation
adnabod to know, to recognise
adnabyddiaeth knowledge
adnabyddir (is/will be) known,
     recognised
adnabyddus well-known
adnau deposit
adnewyddadwy renewable
adnewyddol renewing
adnewyddu to renew, to renovate
adnod verse
adnodd resource
adnoddau resources
adolygiad review
adolygiadau reviews
adolygu to review, to revise
adolygwyd (was) reviewed,
     revised
adran department, section
adrannau sections
adrannol departmental
adre homewards
adref homewards
adrodd to report, to recite,
     to narrate
adroddiad report

adroddiadau reports
adroddir (is/will be) recited,
     reported
adroddodd (he/she/it) recited,
     reported
adroddwyd (was) recited,
     reported
adsefydlu to re-establish,
     to rehabilitate
adwaenir (is) known, recognised
adwaith reaction
adweithiau reactions
adweithio to react
adwerthu to retail
adwy breach, gap
aed (let him/her/it) go
aeddfed mature, ripe
aeddfedrwydd maturity
aeddfedu to mature, to ripen
ael eyebrow
aelod limb, member
aelodaeth membership
aelodau members
aelwyd fireside, household
aelwydydd households
aer[1] air
aer[2] heir
aeth (he/she/it) went
aethant (they) went
aethom (we) went
aethon (they) went
aethpwyd (was) gone, taken
af (I will) go
afael to grasp
afal apple
afalau apples
Affricanaidd African

affrodisaidd aphrodisiacal
afiach unhygienic, unhealthy, ill
afiechyd disease, illness
afiechydon diseases
aflan dirty, unclean
aflonydd restless, uneasy
aflonyddu to disturb, to ruffle
aflonyddwch disquiet, unrest
aflwyddiannus unsuccessful
afon river
afonydd rivers
afreolaidd erratic, irregular
afresymol irrational, unreasonable
afu liver
ag¹ with
ag² as
agenda agenda
agendâu agendas
ager steam
agor to open, to undo
agored open
agoriad key, opening
agoriadol opening
agorodd (he/she/it) opened
agorwch (you) open
agorwyd (was) opened
agos near
agosach nearer
agosaf nearest
agwedd attitude
agweddau attitudes
ai is it, whether
âi (he/she/it would/used to) go
aiff (he/she/it) goes, will go
Aifft Egypt
aig shoal
ail second

ailadeiladu to rebuild
ailadrodd to reiterate, to repeat
ailbrisio to reprice
ailddatblygu to redevelop
ailddefnyddio to reuse
ailgylchu to recycle
ailosod to reset
ailsefydlu to re-establish,
    to reinstate
ailstrwythuro to restructure
ailystyried to reconsider
air word
alaw¹ air, melody
alaw² white water lily
alawon tunes
Alban Scotland
Albanaidd Scottish
albwm album
alcohol alcohol
all (he/she/it) can, is able
allaf (I) am able, can
allai (he/she/it would/used to)
    be able
allan¹ out, outside
allan² (they) are able, can
allanol external, outdoor
allant (they) are able, can
allbwn output
allbynnau outputs
allech (you would/used to)
    be able
allen (they would/used to)
    be able
allent (they would/used to)
    be able
allforio to export
allor altar

allt hill, wood
alltraeth offshore
alltud[1] exile, deportee
alltud[2] exiled
allu to be able
alluoedd abilities, forces
alluog clever
alluogi to enable
allwch (you) are able, can
allwedd clef, key
allweddi keys
allweddol key
allwn (we) are able, can
allyriad emission
allyriadau emissions
allyriannau emissions
allyriant emission
Almaen Germany
Almaeneg German (language)
alw to call
alwad call
alwadau calls
alwedigaeth vocation
alwedigaethol vocational
alwminiwm aluminium
alwodd (he/she/it) called
am[1] because, since
am[2] about, at, for, to, want
amaeth agriculture
amaethu to cultivate
amaethwr farmer
amaethwyr farmers
amaethyddiaeth agriculture
amaethyddol agricultural
amatur amateur
amau to doubt, to suspect
ambell occasional, some

ambiwlans ambulance
amcan intention, notion
amcangyfrif[1] estimate
amcangyfrif[2] to estimate
amcangyfrifedig estimated
amcangyfrifir (is/will be)
   estimated
amcangyfrifon estimates
amcangyfrifwyd (was) estimated
amcanion aims
amcanu to aim, to estimate,
   to intend
amdanaf about me, around me,
   towards me
amdanat about you, around you,
   towards you
amdani about her, around her,
   towards her
amdano about him, around him,
   towards him
amdanoch about you, around
   you, towards you
amdanom about us, around us,
   towards us
amdanyn about them, around
   them, towards them
amdanynt about them, around
   them, towards them
amddifad destitute, orphaned
amddifadedd deprivation,
   destitution
amddiffyn to defend, to protect
amddiffynfa fortress
amddiffynfeydd fortresses
amddiffyniad defence
amddiffynnol defensive,
   protective

amddiffynnwr defender
amen amen
Americanaidd American
Americanwr American
Americanwyr Americans
amgaeedig enclosed
amgáu to enclose, to surround
amgen alternative, different
amgenach better, otherwise
amgueddfa museum
amgueddfeydd museums
amgyffred[1] to comprehend
amgyffred[2] comprehension
amgylch about, around,
   circumcircle
amgylchedd environment
amgylcheddau environments
amgylcheddol environmental
amgylchfyd environment
amgylchiad circumstance, event
amgylchiadau circumstances
amgylchynol surrounding
amgylchynu to surround
amhariad impairment
amharod unprepared, unwilling
amharodrwydd reluctance
amharu to harm, to impair
amhenodol indefinite,
   indeterminate
amherffaith imperfect
amherthnasol irrelevant
amheuaeth doubt, suspicion
amheuir (is/will be) doubted
amheuon doubts
amheus doubtful, dubious
amhosib impossible
amhosibl impossible

amhriodol improper,
   inappropriate
amhrisiadwy invaluable, priceless
aml frequent, many, numerous,
   often
amlach more often
amlaf most often
amlddisgyblaethol
   multidisciplinary
amlder abundance, frequency
amledd frequency
amlen envelope
amlgyfrwng multimedia
amlinelliad outline, sketch
amlinellir (is/will be) outlined
amlinellol outlined
amlinellu to outline
amlinellwyd (was) outlined
amlwg obvious, prominent,
   famous
amlycaf most obvious
amlygiad disclosure, manifestation
amlygrwydd prominence
amlygu to expose, to reveal
amlygwyd (was) revealed
amnewid to replace, to substitute
amod condition
amodau conditions
amodol conditional
amrediad range
amrwd crude, raw
amryfal various
amryliw multicoloured, variegated
amryw[1] sundry, various
amryw[2] diversity, variety
amrywiad variation
amrywiadau variations

amrywiaeth variation, variety
amrywiaethau varieties
amrywio to differ, to vary
amrywiol variable, various
amser[1] tense, time
amser[2] when
amserau times
amseriad tempo, timing
amserlen timetable
amserlenni timetables
amseroedd times
amserol timely
amseru to time
amsugno to absorb
amwynder amenity
amwys ambiguous
amynedd patience
amyneddgar patient
anabl disabled
anabledd disability
anableddau disabilities
anad in preference to, rather than
anaddas inapplicable, unsuitable
anadl breath
anadlu to breathe, to respire
anaf injury
anafiadau injuries
anafu to hurt, to injure
anafwyd (was) injured
anallu inability
analog analogue
anaml infrequent, rare
anarferol unusual
anawsterau difficulties
andwyol harmful, injurious
aned (he/she/it was) born
aneddiadau settlements

aneffeithiol ineffective
aneglur obscure, unclear
anelir (is/will be) aimed
anelu to aim, to draw
anerchiad address, greeting
anfantais detriment, disadvantage
anfanteision disadvantages
anfarwol immortal, unforgettable
anfasnachol uncommercial
anferth huge, vast
anferthol huge
anffafriol unfavourable
anffodus hapless, unfortunate
anffurfiol informal
anfoddhaol unsatisfactory
anfodlon discontented, unwilling
anfodlonrwydd discontent, displeasure
anfon to send, to accompany
anfoneb invoice
anfonebau invoices
anfonir (is/will be) sent
anfonodd (he/she/it) sent
anfonwch (you) send
anfonwyd (was) sent
anfwriadol unintentional
angau death
angel angel
angen need
angenrheidiol necessary
angenrheidrwydd necessity
angerdd force, passion
angerddol intense
anghenion necessities
anghenraid necessity
anghenus needy
angheuol fatal, mortal

anghofio to forget
anghydfod disagreement, dissension
anghydfodau dissensions
anghydraddoldeb inequality
anghydraddoldebau inequalities
anghyfannedd desolate, uninhabited
anghyfartal unequal
anghyfarwydd unaccustomed, unfamiliar
anghyfforddus uncomfortable
anghyffredin uncommon
anghyfiawnder injustice
anghyflawn incomplete, transitive
anghyfleuster inconvenience
anghyfleustra inconvenience
anghyfreithlon illegal, illegitimate, unlawful
anghyfyngedig unrestricted
anghymdeithasol unsociable
anghysbell remote
anghyson fickle, inconsistent
anghysondeb anomaly, inconsistency
anghysonderau anomalies
anghytundeb disagreement
anghytuno to disagree
anghywir incorrect, wrong
angladd funeral
angladdau funerals
Anglicanaidd Anglican
angylion angels
anhapus unhappy
anhawster difficulty
anheddau dwellings, settlements
anheddiad settlement

anheddu to settle
anhepgor indispensable
anhrefn anarchy, confusion
anhwyldeb indisposition, sickness
anhwylder indisposition
anhwylderau illnesses
anhygoel incredible, unbelievable
anhysbys unknown
anial[1] desolate
anial[2] desert, wilderness
anialwch desert, wilderness
anian nature, temperament
anifail animal, beast
anifeiliaid animals
animeiddio to animate
annatod inextricable
annedd dwelling
annerbyniol inadmissible, unacceptable
annerch to address
annhebyg unlike, unlikely
annhebygol improbable, unlikely
annheg unfair
annibyniaeth independence
annibynnol Congregationalist, independent, Independent
annibynwyr independents
annifyr disagreeable, unpleasant
annigonol inadequate, insufficient
annisgwyl unexpected, unforeseen
annog to abet, to exhort, to urge
annomestig non-domestic
annuwiol ungodly
annwyd the common cold

annwyl dear
annymunol undesirable,
    unpleasant
anobaith despair
anochel inescapable, inevitable
anodd difficult, hard
anoddach harder (i.e. more
    difficult)
anogaeth exhortation
anogir (is/will be) urged
anorfod inevitable, invincible
anos more difficult
anrheg gift, present
anrhegion gifts
anrhydedd honour
anrhydeddu to honour
anrhydeddus honorary,
    honourable
ansawdd condition, quality
ansefydlog unstable, unsettled,
    labile
ansicr doubtful, uncertain
ansicrwydd doubt, uncertainty
ansoddair adjective
ansoddeiriau adjectives
ansoddol qualitative
anstatudol non-statutory
anterth peak, prime
anti auntie
antur adventure, venture
anturiaeth adventure
anturiaethau adventures
anuniongyrchol indirect
anwastad fickle, uneven
anweddus indecent, unseemly
anweithredol inactive,
    inoperative

anweledig invisible
anwes[1] fondness
anwes[2] pet
anwiredd falsehood, untruth
anwybodaeth ignorance
anwybyddu to ignore, to snub
anwyd (he/she/it was) born
anymwybodol unaware,
    unconscious
ap son of
apêl appeal
apelau appeals
apeliad appeal
apeliadau appeals
apelio to appeal, to attract
apeliwr appellant
apelydd appellant
apwyntiad appointment
apwyntiadau appointments
ar on, upon, at, about, with
âr tilth
Arabaidd Arabian
aradr plough
araf slow
arafach slower
arafu to retard, to slow (down)
araith speech
arall other
arallgyfeirio to diversify
arbed to salvage, to save
arbedion savings
arbenigedd expertise, specialism
arbenigo to specialise
arbenigol specialised
arbenigwr expert, specialist
arbenigwyr specialists
arbennig distinctive, special

arbrawf experiment
arbrofi to experiment
arbrofion experiments
arbrofol experimental
arch[1] coffin
arch[2] ark
archaeoleg archaeology
archaeolegol archaeological
archdderwydd archdruid
archddiacon archdeacon
archeb order
archebion orders
archebu to order
archeoleg archaeology
archeolegol archaeological
archesgob archbishop
archfarchnad hypermarket,
    supermarket
archfarchnadoedd
    supermarkets
archif archive
archifau archives
archifdy archive office
archifol archival
archwiliad audit, investigation
archwiliadau investigations
archwiliedig audited
archwilio to audit, to examine,
    to explore, to inspect
archwiliwr auditor, examiner
archwiliwyd (was) audited,
    examined
archwilwyr auditors
archwilydd auditor
ardal district
ardaloedd areas
ardd garden

arddangos to exhibit, to reveal
arddangosfa exhibition
arddangosfeydd exhibitions
arddangosiadau exhibitions
arddegau teens
arddel to accept, to
    acknowledge
ardderchog excellent
arddull style
arddulliau styles
ardrethol rateable
ardrethu to tax
ardystiad attestation,
    endorsement
ardystiedig attested
ardystio to attest, to endorse
aredig to plough
aren kidney
arennau kidneys
arestio to arrest
arf tool, weapon
arfaeth God's design, purpose
arfaethedig intended, proposed
arfarniad evaluation
arfarnu to evaluate
arfau arms, weapons
arfer[1] custom, habit
arfer[2] to be used to, to get
    used to
arferadwy accustomed, usual
arferai (he/she/it) used to
arferiad custom
arferion customs
arferol usual
arfog armed
arfor coastal
arfordir coast

arfordirol coastal
argae dam, embankment
argaeledd availability
arglwydd lord, peer (of the realm)
arglwyddes Lady
arglwyddi lords
arglwyddiaeth lordship
argraff impression
argraffadwy impressionable
argraffiad edition, imprint
argraffiadau impressions
argraffu to impress upon, to print
argraffwr printer
argraffwyd (was) printed
argraffydd printer
argyfwng crisis, emergency
argyfyngau crises, emergencies
argyhoeddedig convinced
argyhoeddi to convince
argyhoeddiad conviction
argymell to recommend, to urge
argymhelliad exhortation, recommendation
argymhellion recommendations
argymhellir (is/will be) recommended
argymhellodd (he/she/it) recommended
argymhellwyd (he/she/it was) recommended
arholi to examine
arholiad examination
arholiadau examinations
arholwr examiner
arholwyr examiners

arholydd examiner
arhosiad stay
arhosodd (he/she/it) stayed, waited
arial spirit, verve
arian[1] money
arian[2] silver
Ariannin Argentina
ariannol financial, monetary, pecuniary
ariannu to finance, to fund, to silver
ariannwyd (he/she/it was) financed
ariennir (is/will be) financed
arlein online
ar-lein on-line
arlliw shade, trace, vestige
arllwys to pour
arloesedd innovation
arloesi to innovate, to pioneer
arloesol innovative, pioneering
arlunio to draw, to paint
arlunwyr artists
arlunydd artist
arlwyo to cater, to prepare
arlywydd president
arna' at me, on me, owed by me, with me
arnaf at me, on me, owed by me, with me
arnat at you, on you, owed by you, with you
arni at her, on her, owed by her, with her
arno at him, on him, owed by him, with him

23

arnoch at you, on you, owed by you, with you

arnom at us, on us, owed by us, with us

arnon at us, on us, owed by us, with us

arnyn at them, on them, owed by them, with them

arnynt at them, on them, owed by them, with them

arogl smell

arolwg survey

arolygiad inspection

arolygiadau inspections

arolygiaeth inspectorate, supervision

arolygol supervisory

arolygon inspections

arolygu to inspect, to supervise, to superintend

arolygwr inspector, supervisor

arolygwyd (was) inspected, supervised

arolygwyr inspectors

arolygydd inspector, superintendent, supervisor

aros to remain, to stay, to wait

arswyd terror

arswydus fearful, horrific

arsylw observation

arsylwadau observations

arsylwi to observe

arteffact artefact

arteffactau artefacts

arth bear

arthritis arthritis

artiffisial artificial

artist artist

artistiaid artists

artistig artistic

aruthrol immense, tremendous

arw rough

arwain to lead, to conduct

arweiniad guidance, leadership

arweiniodd (he/she/it) conducted, led

arweiniol introductory, leading

arweinwyr leaders

arweinydd conductor, leader

arweinyddiaeth leadership

arweinyddion conductors

arwerthiant auction

arwr hero

arwydd sign, symbol

arwyddion signs

arwyddo to sign, to signify

arwyddocâd significance

arwyddocaol significant

arwyddwyd (was) signed

arwyneb face, surface

arwynebau surfaces

arwynebedd surface, superficiality

arwynebol superficial

arwyr heroes

arwystl charge (legal)

AS MP

ASau MPs

asbestos asbestos

ased asset

asedau assets

asedion assets

aseiniad assignment

aseiniadau assignments

asesiad assessment
asesiadau assessments
asesir (is/will be) assessed
asesu to assess
aseswr assessor
aseswyd (was) assessed
aseswyr assessors
asesydd assessor
asgell fin, wing
asgwrn bone
Asiaidd Asian
asiant agent
asiantaeth agency
asiantaethau agencies
asiantau agents
asid acid
asidau acids
astud diligent, intent
astudiaeth study
astudiaethau studies
astudio to study
astudir (is/will be) studied
astudiwyd (was) studied
asyn ass
at for, towards, (up) to
ata' to me
ataf to me
atafaelu to distrain, to sequester
atal[1] to prevent, to staunch
atal[2] impediment, stammer
ataliol preventative, repressive
atalnodi to punctuate
atat to you
atborth feedback
ateb[1] to answer, to reply
ateb[2] answer, reply, solution
atebion answers

atebodd (he/she/it) answered
atebol accountable, responsible
atebolrwydd responsibility,
    liability, accountability
atebwch (you) answer
atebwyr respondents
atebydd respondent
ategol ancillary, corroborative
ategu to attach, to confirm,
    to support
atgof reminiscence
atgoffa to remind
atgofion reminiscences
atgyfnerthu to recuperate, to
    reinforce
atgyfodiad resurrection,
    Resurrection
atgynhyrchu to reproduce
atgynhyrchwyd (was)
    reproduced
atgyweiriad repair
atgyweiriadau repairs
atgyweirio to repair, to restore
athrawes schoolmistress,
    teacher
athrawiaeth doctrine
athrawon teachers
athro professor, teacher
athrofa academy, college
athroniaeth philosophy
athronyddol philosophical
athrylith genius
ati to her
atlas atlas
atmosffer atmosphere
ato to him
atoch to you

atodiad appendix, supplement
atodiadau supplements
atodlen schedule
atodol additional, supplementary
atom[1] to us
atom[2] atom
atomau atoms
atyn to them
atyniad attraction
atyniadau attractions
atyniadol attractive, engaging
atynt to them
au false
aur[1] gold
aur[2] golden
awch keenness, sharpness
awdit audit
awdl poem
awdur author
awdurdod authority
awdurdodaeth jurisdiction
awdurdodau authorities
awdurdodedig authorised
awdurdodi to authorise
awdurdodiad authorisation
awdurdodir (is/will be) authorised
awdurdodol authoritative
awdurdodwyd (was) authorised
awdures authoress
awduron authors

awel breeze
awen[1] muse
awen[2] rein
awenau reins
awgrym suggestion
awgryma (he/she/it will) suggest
awgrymiadau suggestions
awgrymir (is/will be) suggested
awgrymodd (he/she/it) suggested
awgrymu to intimate, to suggest
awgrymwyd (was) suggested
awn[1] (we will) go
awn[2] (let's) go!
awn[3] (I would/used to) go
awr hour, time
Awst August
Awstralasia Australasia
Awstralia Australia
Awstria Austria
awtistiaeth autism
awtomatig automatic
awydd desire
awyddus eager
awyr air, sky
awyren aeroplane
awyrennau aeroplanes
awyrgylch atmosphere
awyrlu air force
awyru to air, to ventilate
a.y.b etc.

B : b

a word starting with **b** printed in *italics* means that the root form
of that word begins with **p**, e.g. *babell* root **pabell**

ba¹ baa
ba² how, what, when, which
baban baby
babanod babies
babell tent
babi¹ baby
babi² poppy
bach¹ hinge, hook
bach² small, dear
bachgen boy
bachyn hook
baco tobacco
bacteria bacteria
baddon bath
bae¹ bay
bae² pay, wage
baech (you) were
baent¹ (they) were
baent² paint
bag bag
bagiau bags
baglu to stumble, to trip
bai¹ blame, fault
bai² (he/she/it) were
baich burden, load
balans balance
balch pleased, proud, vain
balchder pleasure, pride
ban¹ place, region
ban² summit
banc bank

banciau banks
bancio to bank
band band
bandiau bands
banel panel
baner flag, pennant
baneri flags
bannau peaks
bant¹ away, off
bant² depression, dip, valley
bapur paper
bapurau papers
bar bar
bâr pair
bara¹ bread
bara² to last
baragraff paragraph
baragraffau paragraphs
baratoi to prepare
baratowyd (was) prepared
barau pairs
barc park
barch respect
barchu to respect
barchus respectable
barcio to park
barcud kite
bardd poet
barddas poetics
barddol bardic, poetic
barddoniaeth poetry

27

barddonol poetic, poetical
bargen bargain
barhad continuation
barhaodd (he/she/it) lasted
barhaol continuous
barhau to continue
barhaus continuous
bariau bars
barn judgement, opinion
barnau judgements
barnu to adjudge, to judge, to think, to try
barnwr judge
barnwriaeth judiciary
barnwrol judicial
barnwyr judges
barod ready
barodd (he/she/it) lasted
barti party
bartïon parties
bartner partner
bartneriaeth partnership
bartneriaethau partnerships
bartneriaid partners
bas¹ shallow
bas² bass
bàs pass
basbort passport
bas dwbl double-bass
basged basket
basio to pass
baswn (I) would have
bath minted, counterfeit
bàth bath
bathodyn badge
batri battery
batrwm pattern

batrymau patterns
baw dirt, excrement
bawb everyone
bawd thumb, big toe
bawn (I) were
Beca Rebecca
bechan¹ little
bechan² little one
bechgyn boys
bechod sin
bechodau sins
becyn package
becynnau packages
bedair four
bedd grave
beddau graves
bedol horseshoe
bedw birch
bedwar four
bedwaredd fourth
bedwerydd fourth
bedydd baptism
bedyddio to baptise, to christen
Bedyddiwr Baptist
Bedyddwyr Baptists
Beibl Bible, Scripture
Beiblaidd Biblical, Scriptural
beic bicycle, bike
beichiau burdens
beichiog burdened, pregnant
beichiogi to cause to be pregnant, to conceive
beichiogrwydd pregnancy
beiciau bicycles
beicio to cycle
beidio to stop
beili¹ bailiff

beili² bailey, farmyard
beilot pilot
beintio to paint
beirdd poets
beiriannau machines
beiriant machine
beirniad adjudicator, critic
beirniadaeth adjudication, criticism
beirniadol critical
beirniadu to adjudicate, to criticise
beirniaid adjudicators
bêl ball
bêl-droed football
belen ball
bell far
bellach any longer, further, later
bellaf furthest
belled as far
bellter distance
ben chief, end, head, mouth, top
benaethiaid heads
benawdau headlines
bencadlys headquarters
bencampwriaeth championship
bendant definite
benderfyniad decision
benderfyniadau decisions
benderfynodd (he/she/it) decided
benderfynol determined
benderfynu to decide
benderfynwyd (was) decided
bendigedig blessed, fantastic, lovely
bendith blessing, grace

bendithion blessings
bennaeth head
bennaf¹ (I/I will) finish
bennaf² primarily
bennill verse
bennir¹ (is/will be) specified
bennir² (is/will be) finished
bennod chapter
bennu¹ to finish
bennu² to specify
bennwyd¹ (was) finished
bennwyd² (was) specified
benodedig specified
benodi to appoint
benodiad appointment
benodiadau appointments
benodir (is/will be) appointed
benodol specific
benodwyd (was) appointed
bensaernïaeth architecture
bensiwn pension
bensiynwyr pensioners
benthyca to borrow, to lend
benthyciad issue, loan
benthyciadau loans
benthyg¹ to borrow
benthyg² borrowed
bentref village
bentrefi villages
benwythnos weekend
benyw female, woman
benywaidd feminine
benywod females, women
ber short
berchen owner
berchennog owner
berchenogion owners

bererindod pilgrimage
berf verb
berfau verbs
berffaith perfect
berfformiad performance
berfformiadau performances
berfformio to perform
beri to cause
bernir (is/will be) judged
berson person, parson
bersonau persons, parsons
bersonél personnel
bersonol personal
bersonoliaeth personality
berswadio to persuade
berthnasau relations
berthnasol relevant
berthyn to belong
berthynai (he/she/it would/
    used to) belong
berthynas relationship
berw[1] boiling, turmoil
berw[2] boiled, boiling
berwi to boil, to go on (about)
berygl danger
beryglon dangers
beryglu to endanger
beryglus dangerous
beth what
bethau things
betio to bet
betrol petrol
betys beet
beudy cowshed
beunydd daily
beunyddiol daily
bicer beaker

bibell pipe
bibellau pipes
bid (let him/her/it) be
big beak
bil bill
biliau bills
biliwn billion
bin[1] bin
bin[2] pen, pin
biniau bins
bioamrywiaeth biodiversity
bioleg biology
biolegol biological
bisgedi biscuits
biwrocratiaeth bureaucracy
bla plague
blaen[1] front, point, tip
blaen[2] plain
blaen[3] (wood) plane
blaenaf foremost
blaenau fronts
blaendal deposit
blaenddalen title page
blaengar progressive, prominent
blaenllaw conspicuous,
    progressive
blaenoriaeth precedence,
    priority
blaenoriaethau priorities
blaenoriaethu to prioritise
blaenorol foregoing, previous
blaid party
blaned planet
blanhigion plants
blanhigyn plant
blannu to plant
blant children

blas¹ taste
blas² palace
blastig plastic
blasu to taste
blasus tasty
blawd flour, meal
ble where
bleidiau parties
bleidlais vote
bleidleisiau votes
bleidleisio to vote
blentyn child
blêr untidy
bleser pleasure
blew hair
blewyn blade of grass, hair,
    whisker
blin cross, sorry
blinder fatigue, tiredness
blinedig tired, tiring
blino to tire, to trouble
blith midst
bloc block
blociau blocks
blodau flowers
blodeuo to flourish, to flower
blodyn flower
bloeddio to shout, to yell
blwch box
blwm lead (metal)
blwydd year(s) old
blwyddlyfr yearbook
blwyddyn year
blwyf parish
blychau boxes
blygu to bend, to fold
blynedd years

blynyddau years
blynyddoedd years
blynyddol annual, yearly
bo (he/she/it) should, may be
bob¹ all, each, every
bob² baked
bobi to bake
bobl people
bobloedd peoples
boblogaeth population
boblogaidd popular
boblogi to populate
boced pocket
boch¹ cheek
boch² (you) should, may be
bocs box, can
bocsys boxes
bod¹ to be, to matter
bod² being, existence
bod³ that
bodau beings
bodd consent, favour, pleasure
boddau pleasure
boddhad gratification, satisfaction
boddhaol satisfactory
boddi to drown, to swamp
bodlon satisfied, willing
bodloni to acquiesce, to satisfy
bodlonrwydd satisfaction
bodolaeth existence
bodolai (he/she/it would/used
    to) exist
bodoli to exist
boed (let him/her/it) be
boen pain
boeni to worry
boenus painful

boeth hot
boi boy
bois boys
bol stomach
bolisi policy
bolisïau policies
bom bomb
bôn base, stem
bond bond
bondiau bonds
bonedd gentry, nobility
boneddigion gentlemen
bonheddig courteous, noble
bont bridge
bonws bonus
bopeth everything
bord table
bore[1] a.m., morning
bore[2] early
boreau mornings
borfa grass
bori to browse, to graze
borth porch, port
bosibiliadau possibilities
bosibilrwydd possibility
bosibl possible
bositif positive
bost[1] boast
bost[2] post
bost[3] complete, utter
bostio[1] to boast
bostio[2] to post
botel bottle
botensial potential
botwm button
botymau buttons
braf ample, fine

braich arm, spoke
braidd[1] hardly, scarcely
braidd[2] congregation, flock
brain crows
braint privilege
brân[1] crow
brân[2] finger-board
bras coarse, fat, general
brasgamu to lope, to stride
braslun sketch
braster fat, richness
brau brittle, fragile
braw fright
brawd[1] brother, friend
brawd[2] friar
brawddeg sentence
brawddegau sentences
brawf proof, test
brawychus terrible
brechdan sandwich, slice of
    bread and butter
brechdanau sandwiches
brechiad inoculation, vaccination
brechu to inoculate, to vaccinate
brecwast breakfast
brefu to low, to moo
bregeth sermon
bregethu to preach
bregus brittle, flimsy
breichiau arms
breifat private
breinio to bless, to favour
bren wood, wooden
brenhines queen, queen-bee
brenhiniaeth realm, reign,
    sovereignty
brenhinoedd kings

brenhinol regal, royal
brenin king
bres brass, money
bresennol present
bresenoldeb presence
brest chest
breswyl residential
breswylwyr residents
breswylydd dweller, resident
breuddwyd day-dream, dream
breuddwydio to day-dream,
    to dream
breuddwydion dreams
bri honour, respect
briciau bricks
brics bricks
bricsen brick
brid breed
bridd soil
bridio to breed
brif main
brifddinas capital city
briff brief
briffio to brief
briffordd main road
brifo to hurt
brifwyl National Eisteddfod
brifysgol university
brifysgolion universities
brig peak, top
brigâd brigade
brigau twigs
brin scarce
brinder scarcity
brint print
brintio to print
briod husband, married, wife

briodas wedding
briodasol wedding
briodi to marry
briodol appropriate
briodoli to attribute
briodweddau characteristics
bris price
brisiau prices
brisio to price, to value
brith[1] abundant
brith[2] dubious, shady
brith[3] mottled, speckled
brith[4] faint
brithyll trout
briw cut, sore, wound
bro region, vale
broblem problem
broblemau problems
brocer[1] broker
brocer[2] poker
brodor native
brodorion natives
brodorol indigenous
brodyr brothers
broffesiynol professional
broffil profile
brofi to experience, to prove
brofiad experience
brofiadau experiences
brofiadol experienced
brofion tests
brofwyd (was) experienced,
    proved
bron[1] breast, heart
bron[2] almost, nearly
bronnau breasts
broses process

33

brosesau processes
brosesu to process
brosiect project
brosiectau projects
brotest protest
brown brown
broydd areas, vales
brwd enthusiastic, heated
brwdfrydedd enthusiasm
brwdfrydig fervent
brwnt dirty, nasty, cruel
Brwsel Brussels
brwsh brush
brwydr battle
brwydrau battles
brwydro to fight
brwyn rushes
Brycheiniog Breconshire
bryd[1] aim, intent
bryd[2] meal
bryd[3] time, when
bryd[4] complexion
brydau meals
bryddest poem
bryder concern
bryderon worries
bryderus concerned
brydferth beautiful
brydferthwch beauty
brydiau[1] aims, intents
brydiau[2] times
brydles lease
brydlon punctual
bryn hill
bryngaer hill-fort
brynhawn afternoon
bryniau hills

brynu to buy
brynwyd (was) bought
brynwyr buyers
brys haste, urgency
Bryste Bristol
brysur busy
bu was, were
buan fast, swift
buarth farmyard, playground
buasai (he/she/it) would have
buaswn (I) would have
buches herd
buchod cows
budd benefit
budd-dal benefit
budd-daliadau benefits
budd-ddeiliad stakeholder
budd-ddeiliaid stakeholders
buddiannau interests, welfare
buddiant interest
buddiol beneficial
buddiolwr beneficiary
buddiolwyr beneficiaries
buddion benefits
buddsoddi to invest
buddsoddiad investment
buddsoddiadau investments
buddsoddwr investor
buddsoddwyr investors
buddugol victorious
buddugoliaeth victory
budr dirty, smutty
bugail pastor, shepherd
bugeiliaid shepherds
bugeiliol pastoral
bum five
bûm (I) was

bumed fifth
bump five
bunnau pounds
bunnoedd pounds
bunt pound
buoch (you) were
buodd was, were
buom (we) were
buont (they) were
bur pure
burum yeast
busnes business
busnesau businesses
buwch cow
bwa arch, bow
bwerau powers
bwlch gap, pass, embrasure
bwled bullet
bwletin bulletin
bwlio to bully
bwll[1] pond, pool
bwll[2] coal-mine, pit
bwnc subject
bwrdd board, table
bwrdeistref borough, municipality
bwriad intention
bwriadau intentions
bwriadol intentional
bwriadu to intend
bwriadwn (we) intend
bwriadwyd (was) intended
bwriedir (is) intended
bwrlwm bubble, bubbling
bwrpas purpose
bwrpasau purposes
bwrpasol purposely
bwrw[1] to rain, to snow

bwrw[2] to hit
bws bus, omnibus
bwthyn cottage
bwy who, whom
bwyd food, victuals
bwydlen menu
bwydlysyddiaeth vegetarianism
bwydo to feed
bwydydd foodstuffs
bwyllgor committee
bwyllgorau committees
bwynt point
bwyntiau points
bwys[1] pound (weight)
bwys[2] emphasis, importance
bwys[3] near
bwysau pounds, pressure, weight
bwysicach more important
bwysicaf most important
bwysig important
bwysigrwydd importance
bwyslais emphasis
bwysleisio to emphasise
bwyso to weigh
bwyta to eat
bwytai cafes, restaurants
bwyty café, restaurant
bychain little, small
bychan[1] little, small
bychan[2] little one
byd Earth, world
bydd will, will be, (you) be!
bydda (I) will, shall
byddaf (I) will, shall
byddai (he/she/it) used to, would
byddan (they) will

35

byddant (they) will

byddar deaf

bydde (he/she/it) used to, would

byddech (you) used to, would

bydded (let him/her/it) be

byddem (we) used to, would

bydden (they) used to, would

byddent (they) used to, would

byddi (you) will

byddid (there) would be, used to be

byddin army

byddo (he/she/it) should

byddwch (you) be!, will

byddwn[1] (we) shall, will

byddwn[2] (I) used to, would

byd-eang global, universal, worldwide

bydol worldly

bydwragedd midwives

bydwraig midwife

bydwreigiaeth midwifery

bydysawd universe

bygwth to threaten

bygythiad menace, threat

bygythiadau threats

bygythiol menacing

bylchau gaps

byllau pits, pools

bymtheg fifteen

bymthegfed fifteenth

bynciau subjects

bynnag (what)soever, (where)soever, (who)soever

byr short

byrddau boards, tables

byrder brevity, shortness

byrion short

byrrach shorter

bys[1] finger, hand (of clock or watch), toe, latch

bys[2] peas

bysedd fingers

bysellfwrdd keyboard

bysgod fishes

bysgodfeydd fisheries

bysgota to fish

bysgotwyr fishermen

bysiau buses

bysus buses

byth always, ever, never

bythefnos fortnight

bythynnod cottages

bytiau snippets

byw[1] to live

byw[2] alive, live, lively, living

byw[3] quick

bywiog lively, vivacious

bywoliaeth benefice, livelihood, living

bywyd life, lifetime, verve

bywydau lives

bywydeg biology

C : c

a word starting with **ch** printed in *italics* means that the root form
of that word begins with **c**, e.g. *chadarn* root **cadarn**

in a Welsh dictionary, unlike this list, **ch** is a letter in its own right and
follows *cy* and precedes *d* alphabetically

c penny, pence, p
caban cabin
cabidwl chapter, conclave
cabinet cabinet
cadair chair, udder
cadarn firm, strong
cadarnhad confirmation
cadarnhaodd (he/she/it)
    confirmed
cadarnhaol affirmative, positive
cadarnhau to confirm, to ratify
cadarnhawyd (was) confirmed
cadeiriau chairs
cadeirio to chair
cadeiriol chaired
cadeirlan cathedral
cadeirydd chairman,
    chairperson
cadeiryddiaeth chairmanship
cadeiryddion chairpersons
cadernid strength
cadi sissy
cadw[1] to keep, to observe,
    to save
cadw[2] reserved
cadw[3] (you) keep!
cadwch (you) keep
cadwedig saved

cadwraeth conservation, custody
cadwraethol conservational
cadwyd (was) kept
cadwyn chain
cadwyni chains
cae field, enclosure
caead lid, shutter
caeau fields
caeedig closed, shut
caeëdig closed, shut
cael to have, to receive,
    to discover, to be allowed
caer castle, fort, rampart
Caerdydd Cardiff
caeth addicted, captive, confined
caethiwed addiction, captivity
caf (I/I will) be allowed, have
caffael to acquire
caffaeliad acquisition
caffe café
caffi café
cafodd (he/she/it) had, was
    allowed
cafwyd (was) allowed, had
câi (he/she/it would/used to) be
    allowed, have
caiff (he/she/it will) be allowed,
    have

cain fine, stylish
cainc branch, knot
cais[1] attempt, effort, request
cais[2] try
cal penis
calan New Year's Day, first day (of)
calch lime, quicklime
calchfaen limestone
caled difficult, hard
caledi adversity, hardship
caledwedd hardware
calendr calendar
Calfinaidd Calvinistic
call sensible, smart
calon heart, core
calonnau hearts
calonogol encouraging, heartening
cam[1] footprint, step
cam[2] wrong
cam[3] bent, crooked, incorrect
cam[4] cam
camarweiniol misleading
camau[1] steps
camau[2] wrongs
camddefnyddio to abuse, to misuse
cam-drin to abuse, to ill-treat
camdriniaeth abuse, ill-treatment
camera camera
camerâu cameras
camfa stile
camgymeriad mistake
camgymeriadau mistakes
camlas canal, channel
camlesi canals
camp feat, game

campau feats
camp lawn grand slam
campws campus
camu[1] to pace, to step
camu[2] to bend, to distort
camweinyddu to maladminister
camymddwyn to misbehave
can hundred
cân[1] lyric, poem, song
cân[2] (he/she/it) sings
cancr cancer, canker
caneuon songs
canfod to discern, to perceive
canfu (he/she/it) discovered, perceived
canfuwyd (was) discovered, perceived
canfyddiad perception
canfyddiadau perceptions
cangen bough, branch
canghellor chancellor
canghennau branches
canhwyllau candles
caniatâ (he/she/it) allows, permits
caniatâd permission
caniataol granted
caniatáu to grant, to permit
caniateir (is/will be) allowed, permitted
canllaw guideline, handrail
canllawiau guidelines
canlyn to court, to follow
canlyniad consequence, result
canlyniadau results
canlyniadol resultant
canlynol following
canmlwyddiant centenary

canmol to pat, to praise
canmoliaeth praise
cannoedd hundreds
cannwyll candle
canodd (he/she/it) sang
canol centre, middle, midriff
canolbarth midlands
canolbwynt essence, focus
canolbwyntio to concentrate
canoldir inland region,
   Mediterranean
canolfan centre
canolfannau centres
canoli to centralise, to mediate
canolig mediocre, middling,
   moderate
canoloesol medieval
canolog basic, central
canolwr centre, intermediary,
   middleman
canon¹ canon
canon² cannon
canran per cent, percentage
canrannau percentages
canrif century
canrifoedd centuries
canser cancer
canslo to cancel
cant hundred, hundredweight
cânt (they/they will) have
cantorion singers
canu¹ to sing, to ring, to play
canu² poem, singing
canwr player, singer
canwyd (was) sung
canys because, since
cap cap

capel chapel
capeli chapels
capten captain
car car
câr kinsman, relative
carafán caravan
carafannau caravans
carbon carbon
carchar gaol, jail, prison
carchardai prisons
carcharor captive, prisoner
carcharorion prisoners
cardiau cards
caredig kind
caredigrwydd kindliness,
   kindness
carfan faction, squad
cariad love, lover, sweetheart
cariadon lovers
cario to bear, to carry
carlamu to gallop
carol carol
carolau carols
carped carpet
carreg pip, stone
carthffosiaeth drainage,
   sewerage
carthion excrement
cartref home
cartrefi homes
cartrefol at home, homely
caru to love
cas¹ hateful, nasty
cas² case
casgliad¹ collection, gathering
casgliad² conclusion
casgliad³ abscess

casgliadau[1] collections, gatherings
casgliadau[2] conclusions
casglu[1] to collect, to congregate
casglu[2] to conclude
casglu[3] to fester
casglwyd[1] (was) collected, gathered
casglwyd[2] (was) concluded
Casnewydd Newport
cast[1] cast, prank, trick
cast[2] caste
castell castle, rook
catalog catalogue
categori category
categorïau categories
cath cat
cathod cats
Catholig Roman Catholic
Catholigion Roman Catholics
cau[1] to close, to fasten, to shut
cau[2] hollow
cawell basket, cradle
cawl[1] broth, soup
cawl[2] mess
cawn[1] (we will) be allowed, have
cawn[2] reeds, stubble
cawod shower, mildew
cawr giant
caws cheese
cawsai (he/she/it) had, was allowed
cawsant (they) had, were allowed
cawsoch (you) had, were allowed
cawsom (we) had, were allowed
cawson (they) had, were allowed
cebl cable

ceblau cables
cedwir (is/will be) kept
cedyrn strong
cefais (I) had, was allowed
ceffyl horse
ceffylau horses
cefn back, rear, reverse
cefnau backs
cefndir background, setting
cefndiroedd backgrounds
cefni (you) desert, withdraw
cefnog wealthy, well-off, well-to-do
cefnogaeth backing, support
cefnogi to support, to second, to encourage
cefnogir (is/will be) supported
cefnogol encouraging, supportive
cefnogwr supporter
cefnogwyr supporters
cefnu to desert, to withdraw
ceg mouth
cegin kitchen
cei[1] (you will) be allowed, have
cei[2] quay
ceid (would be/used to be) had, allowed
ceidwad keeper
ceidwadol conservative, Conservative
ceidwadwr conservative
ceidwadwyr conservatives
ceiliog cockerel
ceiniog penny
ceir[1] cars
ceir[2] (is to be) allowed, had

ceirch oats
ceirw deer
ceisiadau requests
ceisio to attempt, to seek, to try
ceisiodd (he/she/it) attempted
ceisiwch (you) attempt
ceiswyr seekers
ceisydd applicant
celf art
celfi furniture, implements
celfydd skilful
celfyddyd art
celfyddydau arts
celfyddydol artistic
cell cell
celli copse, grove
celloedd cells
Celt Celt
Celtaidd Celtic
Celtiaid Celts
celwydd lie
celyn holly
cemeg chemistry
cemegau chemicals
cemegol chemical
cen dandruff, lichen, scale
cenedl[1] nation
cenedl[2] gender
cenedlaethau generations
cenedlaethol national, nationalist
cenedlaetholdeb nationalism
cenedligrwydd nationhood
cenhadaeth mission
cenhedlaeth generation
cenhedloedd nations
cenhedlu to beget, to procreate
cer (you) go!

cerbyd carriage, vehicle
cerbydau carriages, vehicles
cerdd music, poem
cerdded to move on, to walk
cerddi poems
cerddodd (he/she/it) walked
cerddor musician
cerddorfa orchestra
cerddoriaeth music
cerddorion musicians
cerddorol musical
cerddwr pedestrian, walker
cerddwyr pedestrians, walkers
cerdyn card
cerflun sculpture, statue
cerrig stones
cerrynt current
ces (I) had, was allowed
cesglir (is/will be) collected
cestyll castles
cewc[1] regard, esteem
cewc[2] peep
cewch (you will) be allowed,
   have
chadarn mighty, strong
chadarnhau to confirm
chadeirydd chairman
chadw to keep
chadwraeth conservation
chaeau fields
chael to be allowed, to have
chaer fort
chafodd (he/she/it) had, was
   allowed
chafwyd (was) allowed, had
chaiff (he/she/it will) be allowed,
   have

chais request
chalon heart
cham pace, step
chamau steps
chamddefnyddio to misuse
chan[1] by, from, have, of, with
chan[2] hundred
chân song
chanddi by her, from her/it, of her/it, she has, with her
chanddo by him, from him/it, he has, of him/it, with him
chanddynt by them, from them, of them, they have, with them
chanfod to perceive
chaniatâd permission
chaniatáu to permit
chaniateir (is/will be) allowed, permitted
chanllawiau guidelines, handrails
chanlyniad result
chanlyniadau results
chanol centre, middle
chanolbarth midland
chanolbwyntio to centre, to focus
chanolfan centre
chanolfannau centres
chanolig middling
chanser cancer
chant hundred
chânt (they/they will) have
chanu to sing
chap cap
char car
chardiau cards
chariad love
chartref home

chartrefi homes
chasgliad conclusion
chasgliadau conclusions
chasglu to collect
chastell castle, rook
chau to close
chawn (we/we will) be allowed, have
chawsant (they) had, were allowed
chawsom (we) had, were allowed
chdi you
chedwir (is/will be) kept
chefais (I) had, was allowed
chefn back
chefndir background
chefnogaeth support
chefnogi to support
cheg mouth
cheir[1] cars
cheir[2] (is to be) allowed, had
cheisiadau requests
cheisio to seek
chenedl[1] nation
chenedl[2] gender
chenedlaethol national
cherbydau carriages, vehicles
cherdded to walk
cherddi poems
cherddoriaeth music
cherrig pips, stones
chewch (you will) be allowed, have
chi[1] you
   chi'ch you your
chi[2] dog
chi'ch you your
chig meat

chithau yourselves
chladdu to bury
chlefyd disease, fever
chleifion patients
chludiant transport
chludo to carry, to transport
chlybiau clubs
chlywed to hear
chlywodd (he/she/it) heard
chodi to lift, to raise
chodir (is/will be) raised
chododd (he/she/it) raised
choed trees, wood
choedwigaeth forestry
choetiroedd woodlands
chofio to remember
chofnodi to record
chofnodion minutes, records
chofrestru to register
chôl embrace, lap
choleg college
cholegau colleges
cholledion losses
cholli to lose
chontractwyr contractors
chopi copy
chorff body
chost cost
chostau costs
chredu to believe
chrefft craft
chrefydd religion
chrefyddol religious
chreu to create
chriw crew
chronfeydd reserves, reservoirs
chryfhau to strengthen

chryn quite
chwaer sister
chwaeth taste
chwaith either, neither
chwalu to destroy, to disintegrate, to scatter
chwaneg more
chwant appetite, desire, lust
chwarae to play
chwaraeodd (he/she/it) payed
chwaraeon games, sports
chwaraewch (you) play
chwaraewr actor, player, sportsman
chwaraewyr actors, players, sportsmen
chwarel quarry
chwareli quarries
chwarelwyr quarrymen
chwartel quartile
chwarter quarter
chwarterol quarterly
chwblhau to complete
chwe six
chwech six
chweched sixth
chwedegau sixties
chwedl[1] fable, story, tale
chwedl[2] so says, according to
chwedlau tales
chwedlonol fabulous, legendary, mythical
Chwefror February
chweil (worth) while
chwerthin[1] to laugh
chwerthin[2] laugh, laughter
chwerw acrid, bitter

43

chwestiwn question
chwestiynau questions
chwi you
chwifio to brandish, to wave
chwilen[1] beetle
chwilen[2] bee in one's bonnet
chwilfrydedd curiosity
chwiliad search
chwiliadau searches
chwilio to search, to examine
chwiliwch (you) search
chwilod beetles
chwilota to rummage, to search
chwim fleet, nimble, swift
chwiorydd sisters
chwisiau quizzes
chwistrellu to inject, to spray, to squirt
chwith[1] amiss, awkward, offended, sad, strange
chwith[2] left
chwithau even you, you on the other hand, you too
chwithig clumsy, strange
chwm valley
chwmni company
chwmnïau companies
chwmpas compass
chwrdd[1] meeting, service
chwrdd[2] to meet, to touch
chwrs[1] chase
chwrs[2] course
chwrs[3] coarse
chwsmeriaid customers
chwyddiant distension, inflation
chwyddo to become puffed up, to swell, to zoom

chwyldro revolution
chwyldroadol revolutionary
chwyn weeds
chwynion complaints
chwyrn heated, vigorous
chwyrnu to snore
chwys perspiration, sweat
chwythu to blow, to blow up, to puff
chychwyn to start
chyd together
chyda with
chydag with
chydlynu to coordinate
chydnabod to acknowledge
chydsyniad agreement
chydweithio to cooperate
chydweithrediad cooperation
chydweithwyr colleagues
chydymffurfio to conform
chyfanrwydd entirety
chyfansoddi to compose
chyfansoddiad composition
chyfanswm total
chyfarfod meeting
chyfarfodydd meetings
chyfarpar equipment
chyfartaledd average, proportion
chyfarwyddiadau directions
chyfarwyddwr director
chyfarwyddyd direction, instruction
chyfathrebu to communicate
chyfeillion friends
chyfeiriad address, direction
chyfeiriadau addresses, directions
chyfeirio to direct

chyfer[1] acre
chyfer[1] behalf
chyfer[1] headlong
chyffro excitement
chyffrous exciting
chyffuriau drugs
chyfiawnder justice
chyfiawnhau to justify
chyfieithu to translate
chyflawni to complete
chyfle opportunity
chyflenwi to supply
chyflenwyr suppliers
chyfleoedd opportunities
chyfleu to convey
chyfleus convenient
chyfleusterau conveniences,
    facilities
chyflog wage
chyflogaeth employment
chyflogau wages
chyflogi to employ
chyflogwyr employers
chyflwr condition
chyflwyniad presentation
chyflwyno to present
chyflwynwyd (was) presented
chyfnewid to exchange
chyfnod period
chyfnodau periods
chyfoes contemporary
chyfoeth wealth
chyfradd rate
chyfraddau rates
chyfraith law
chyfran share
chyfraniad contribution

chyfraniadau contributions
chyfrannu to contribute
chyfranogiad participation
chyfreithiwr lawyer
chyfres series
chyfrif account
chyfrifoldeb responsibility
chyfrifoldebau duties,
    responsibilities
chyfrifon accounts
chyfrinach secret
chyfryngau media
chyfyngiadau restrictions
chyfyngu to restrict
chyhoeddi to announce, to publish
chyhoeddiadau publication
chyhoeddus public
chyhoeddusrwydd publicity
chyhoeddwyd (was) announced,
    published
chylch circle
chylchgronau magazines
chyllid finance
chyllido to finance
chymaint as much
chymdeithas society
chymdeithasau societies
chymdeithasol social
chymeradwyo to recommend
chymeriad character
chymeriadau characters
chymerodd (he/she/it) took
chymerwyd (was) taken
chymharu to compare
chymhelliant motivation, motive
chymhleth complex
chymhwyso to adjust

chymhwyster qualification
chymorth help, support
Chymraeg Welsh
Chymreig Welsh
Chymru Wales
chymryd to take
chymuned community
chymunedau communities
chymunedol community
chymwysterau qualifications
chyn as, before, so
chynefinoedd habitats
chynghorau councils
chynghori to advise
chynghorwyr advisers, councillors
chynghorydd advisor, councillor
chyngor advice, council
chynhaliaeth support, sustenance
chynhaliwyd (was) held
chynhelir (is/will be) held
chynhwysfawr comprehensive
chynhwysir (is/will be) included
chynhyrchion products
chynhyrchu to produce
chynigion attempts, proposals
chynllun plan
chynlluniau plans
chynllunio to plan
chynnal to support
chynnig offer, proposal, try
chynnwys[1] content, contents
chynnwys[2] to include, to contain, to consist
chynnydd increase
chynnyrch produce, product
chynorthwyo to support
chynrychiolaeth representation

chynrychiolwyr representatives
chynrychiolydd representative
chynulliad assembly, group
chynyddu to increase
chyrff bodies
chyrhaeddiad reach
chyrraedd to arrive
chyrsiau courses
chysgu to sleep
chyson constant
chysondeb consistency
chyswllt contact
chysylltiad link
chysylltiadau contacts
chysylltu to link
chytundeb agreement, contract
chytundebau agreements, contracts
chytuno to agree
chytunwyd (was) agreed
chywir correct
chywirdeb accuracy
ci dog
cic kick
cicio to kick
cig meat
cil nook, retreat
cilio to recede, to retreat, to withdraw
cilomedr kilometre
cinio dinner, lunch
cip glimpse
cipio to snatch, to win
cipolwg glance, glimpse
cist chest, coffin
ciwbig cubic, cubical
claddfa cemetery, graveyard

claddu to bury, to inter
claddwyd (was) buried
claf[1] ill, sick
claf[2] invalid, patient
clai clay
clas cloister
clasurol classic, classical
clawdd ditch, hedge
clawr cover, lid, surface
clebran to chatter, to gossip
clecs gossip
cleddyf sword, cleat
clefyd disease, illness, infection
clefydau diseases
cleient client
cleientau clients
cleientiaid clients
cleifion patients
clerc clerk
clicio to click
cliciwch (you) click
clinic clinic
clinig clinic
clinigau clinics
clinigol clinical
clir clear, net (profit etc.)
cliriach clearer
clirio to clear
clo conclusion, lock
cloc clock, speedometer
cloch bell, bubble, o'clock
clod credit, praise
cloddiau hedges
cloddio to dig, to excavate
clogwyn boulder, cliff, precipice
clogwyni cliffs
cloi to conclude, to end, to lock

clos enclosure, farmyard
clòs close, near
cludiant transport
cludir (is/will be) carried, transported
cludo to carry, to convey, to transport
clust ear
clustiau ears
clustnodi to earmark
clwb club
clwstwr cluster
clwy disease, sore, wound
clwyf disease, sore, wound
clybiau clubs
clychau bells
clyd cosy, snug
clymu to bind, to knot, to tie
clystyrau clusters
clyw[1] earshot, hearing
clyw[2] (you) listen!
clyw[3] (he/she/it) hears
clywais (I) heard
clywch (you) hear
clywed to hear
clywedol auditory, aural
clywodd (he/she/it) heard
cm cm
cnau nuts
cnawd flesh
cnewyllol nuclear
cnewyllyn core, kernel
cnoi to bite, to chew
cnwd covering, crop
cnydau crops
'co look!
co' memory

còb¹ lad, wag
còb² cob (horse)
còb³ embankment
coch¹ red, ginger, auburn, brown
coch² poor, ropy, lewd
cochion red, reds
cocos¹ cockles
cocos² cogs
cod¹ bag, pod
cod² code
codau codes
codi to raise, to lift, to build, to get up
codiad erection, increase
codir (is/will be) raised
cododd (he/she/it) raised
codwyd (was) raised
coed trees
coeden tree
coediog sylvan, wooded
coedwig forest, wood
coedwigaeth forestry
coedwigoedd forests
coes¹ leg
coes² handle, stalk, stem
coesau legs
coetir woodland
coetiroedd woodlands
cof memory
cofeb memorial
coffa memorial, remembrance
coffi coffee
cofia (you) remember!
cofiadwy memorable
cofiaf (I/I will) remember
cofio to recall, to remember
cofiwch (you) remember

cofnod memorandum, minute, record
cofnodi to minute, to record, to register
cofnodion minutes, records
cofnodir (is/will be) recorded
cofnodwyd (was) recorded
cofrestr register
cofrestra (he/she/it will) register
cofrestrau registers
cofrestredig registered
cofrestrfa registry
cofrestri (you) register
cofrestriad registrations
cofrestriadau registrations
cofrestru to register, to enrol
cofrestrwyd (was) registered
cofrestrydd registrar
coginio to cook
côl embrace, lap
colect collect
coleg college
colegau colleges
coler band, collar
coll lost, missing
collddail deciduous
colled loss, insanity
colledion losses
colli to lose, to miss, to spill
collir (is/will be) lost
collodd (he/she/it) lost
collwyd (was) lost
colofn column, pillar
colofnau columns
comedi comedy
comin common
comisiwn commission

comisiynu to commission
comisiynwr commissioner
comisiynwyd (was) commissioned
comisiynwyr commissioners
comisiynydd commissioner
compostio to compost
condemnio to condemn
confensiwn convention
confensiynau conventions
confensiynol conventional
consensws consensus
consortiwm consortium
contract contract
contractau contracts
contractio to contract
contractiwr contractor
contractwr contractor
contractwyr contractors
copa peak, summit, crown, pate
copi copy
copïau copies
copïo to copy, to imitate
copïwch (you) copy
copr copper
cor[1] dwarf, midget, pygmy
cor[2] spider
côr chancel, choir, pew
corau choirs
corddi to churn, to seethe, to stir
corff body, group
corfforaeth corporation
corfforaethol corporate
corfforol bodily, physical
coridor corridor
coridorau corridors
corn[1] horn, trumpet, antler, callous

corn[2] horn, antler, callous
corn[3] maize
corn[4] absolute, complete
cornel corner
coron crown, garland
coronaidd coronary
cors bog, marsh
corsydd bogs
cosb penalty, punishment
cosbau punishments
cosbi to penalise, to punish
cosi to itch
cost cost
costau costs
costio to cost
costus dear, expensive
cot coat, coating
côt coat, coating
cotwm cotton
cownter counter
crac angry, annoyed
craff sharp, shrewd
craffu to observe, to pore, to scrutinise
crafu to peel, to scrape, to scratch
cragen shell
crai crude, raw
craidd centre, crux, essence
craig boulder, crag, rock
crand grand, smart
cras aired, baked, coarse, rough
creadigaeth creation, procreation, the creation
creadigol created, creative
creadur creature
creaduriaid creatures
cred belief, Christendom, trust

credaf (I) believe
credai (he/she/it would/used to) believe
credir (is/will be) believed
credo credo, creed
credoau creeds
credu to believe
credwch (you) believe
credwn (we) believe
credyd credit
credydau credits
credydwr creditor
credydwyr creditors
cref strong
crefft craft, trade
crefftau crafts
crefftwr craftsman
crefftwyr craftsmen
crefydd religion
crefyddol religious
cregyn shell
creiddiol core, central, essential
creigiau rocks
creigiog craggy, rocky
creision crisps, flakes
creodd (he/she/it) created
creu to create, to make
creulon brutal, cruel, heartless
creulondeb brutality, cruelty
crëwyd (was) created
crib comb, crest
criced cricket
crio to cry
Crist Christ
Cristion Christian
Cristnogaeth Christianity
Cristnogion Christians

Cristnogol Christian
critigol critical
criw crew, gang
croen hide, peel, skin
croes[1] cross, crucifix
croes[2] adverse, against, cross
croesawodd (he/she/it) welcomed
croesawu to welcome
croesawyd (was) welcomed
croesfan crossing
croesi to cross, to traverse
croeso hospitality, welcome
crogi to hang
cromfach bracket (round), parenthesis
cromfachau parentheses, brackets
cron circular, round
cronedig accumulated
cronfa fund, reservoir
cronfeydd funds, reservoirs
cronig chronic
cronni to amass, to dam up
croth uterus, womb
croyw fresh, pure, unleavened
crwn circular, entire, round
crwner coroner
crwydro to stray, to wander
crybwyll to mention, to refer to
crybwyllir (is/will be) mentioned
crybwyllwyd (was) mentioned
cryf powerful, strong
cryfach stronger
cryfaf strongest
cryfder might, power, strength

cryfderau strengths
cryfhau to grow powerful, to strengthen
cryfion strong
cryn quite, fair, pretty, tolerable
crynhoad[1] gathering, accumulation
crynhoad[2] summary
crynhoi[1] to assemble, to accumulate
crynhoi[2] to summarise
crynhoi[3] to fester
cryno compact, concise
crynoadau compendia
crynodeb abstract, résumé, summary
crynodiad concentration
crynodiadau concentrations
crynswth entirety, gross
crynu to shiver, to tremble
crys shirt
crysau shirts
cu beloved, dear
cudd hidden, secret
cuddio to conceal, to hide, to obscure
cul narrow, narrow-minded
curo to beat, to knock
cwbl[1] everything
cwbl[2] total, entire, whole, complete
cwblhau to complete, to finish
cwblhawyd (was) completed
cwblhewch (you) complete
cwbwl[1] everything
cwbwl[2] total, entire, whole, complete

cwch boat, hive
cwest inquest
cwestiwn question
cwestiynau questions
cwis quiz
cwisiau quizzes
cwlwm cluster, knot, tangle
cwm coomb, glen, valley
cwmni companions, companionship, company
cwmnïau companies
cwmpas[1] compass, scope
cwmpas[2] pair of compasses
cwmpasu to encompass
cwmwl cloud
cŵn dogs
cwningen rabbit
cwningod rabbits
cwnstabl constable
cwota quota
cwpan capsule, chalice, cup
cwpled couplet
cwpwl couple
cwpwrdd cupboard
cwr corner, edge, outskirts
cwrdd[1] meeting, service
cwrdd[2] to meet, to touch
cwricwlaidd curricular
cwricwlwm curriculum
cwrlid blanket, coverlet
cwrs[1] chase
cwrs[2] course
cwrs[3] coarse
cwrt court, courtroom
cwrtais courteous
cwrw ale, beer
cwsg sleep

cwsmer customer
cwsmeriaid customers
cwstard custard
cwt[1] cot, hut, shanty
cwt[2] tail, tang
cwt[3] cut
cwtogi to contract, to shorten, to shrink
cwtsio to snuggle up
cwymp collapse, fall
cwympo to fall, to slope down
cwyn accusation, complaint
cwynion complaints
cwyno to complain
cwynodd (he/she/it) complained
cychod boats
cychwyn[1] beginning, start
cychwyn[2] to start, to begin, to depart
cychwynnodd (he/she/it) started
cychwynnol initial
cychwynnwyd (was) started
cyd joining, union
cydau bags
cydbwysedd balance, equilibrium
cydbwyso to balance, to weigh
cyd-destun context
cyd-destunau contexts
cyd-fynd to agree
cydgysylltu to coordinate
cydio to hold, to hold fast, to seize
cydlynol cohesive
cydlynu to cohere, to coordinate
cydlynus coordinative
cydlynydd coordinator
cydnabod[1] to acknowledge, to show appreciation

cydnabod[2] acquaintance
cydnabuwyd (was) acknowledged
cydnabyddedig acknowledged, recognised
cydnabyddiaeth acknowledgement, appreciation
cydnabyddir (is/will be) acknowledged
cydnaws compatible, congenial
cydol the whole
cydradd equal
cydraddoldeb equality
cydran component
cydrannau components
cydsyniad agreement, consent
cydsynio to agree, to assent
cydweddu to conform
cydweithio to collaborate, to cooperate
cydweithiwr colleague
cydweithrediad collaboration, cooperation
cydweithredol collaborative, cooperative
cydweithredu to cooperate
cydweithwyr colleagues
cydwybod conscience
cydymdeimlad commiseration, sympathy
cydymdeimlo to commiserate, to sympathise
cydymffurfiad compliance
cydymffurfiaeth conformity
cydymffurfio to conform
cyf.[1] ltd.
cyf.[2] ref.
cyf.[3] vol.

cyfaddas suitable
cyfaddef to admit, to confess
cyfadran faculty
cyfadrannau faculties
cyfagos adjoining, close
cyfaill friend
cyfaint volume
cyfalaf capital
cyfamod covenant
cyfamser meantime, meanwhile
cyfan[1] complete, whole
cyfan[2] total, whole
cyfandir continent
cyfannol holistic, integral, integrated
cyfanrwydd totality, wholeness
cyfansawdd compound
cyfansoddi to compose
cyfansoddiad composition, constitution
cyfansoddiadol constitutional
cyfansoddion compounds
cyfansoddol component
cyfansoddwr composer
cyfanswm sum, total
cyfansymiau totals
cyfarch[1] address, greeting
cyfarch[2] to greet
cyfarfod[1] meeting
cyfarfod[2] to meet, to touch
cyfarfodydd meetings
cyfarpar apparatus, equipment
cyfartal equal
cyfartaledd average, proportion
cyfartalog average
cyfarwydd[1] familiar
cyfarwydd[2] raconteur, storyteller

cyfarwyddeb directive
cyfarwyddiadau directions
cyfarwyddiaeth directorship
cyfarwyddo[1] to direct
cyfarwyddo[2] to become accustomed to
cyfarwyddwr director
cyfarwyddwraig director (female)
cyfarwyddwyr directors
cyfarwyddyd advice, instruction
cyfateb to correspond, to tally
cyfatebol corresponding
cyfathrach intercourse
cyfathrebu to communicate
cyfeillgar amicable, friendly
cyfeillgarwch friendliness, friendship
cyfeillion friends
cyfeiriad[1] address, reference
cyfeiriad[2] direction
cyfeiriadau[1] addresses, references
cyfeiriadau[2] directions
cyfeiriadur directory
cyfeirio[1] to refer
cyfeirio[2] to direct
cyfeiriodd[1] (he/she/it) referred
cyfeiriodd[2] (he/she/it) directed
cyfeirir[1] (is/will be) referred
cyfeirir[2] (is/will be) directed
cyfeiriwyd[1] (was) referred
cyfeiriwyd[2] (was) directed
cyfeirlyfr reference book
cyfeirnod grid reference, reference
cyfenw surname

cyfer acre
cyferbyn opposite
cyferbyniad contrast
cyffelyb like, such
cyffiniau bounds, vicinity
cyffordd junction
cyfforddus comfortable
cyffredin common, ordinary
cyffredinol general, universal
cyffro commotion, excitement,
   stir
cyffroi to agitate, to stir
cyffrous agitated, exciting
cyffur drug
cyffuriau drugs
cyffwrdd to touch
cyfiawn just, righteous
cyfiawnder justice, righteousness
cyfiawnhad justification,
   vindication
cyfiawnhau to justify, to
   vindicate
cyfieithiad translation
cyfieithiadau translations
cyfieithu to translate
cyfieithwyr translators
cyfieithydd interpreter, translator
cyflawn[1] complete, full
cyflawn[2] intransitive
cyflawni to accomplish, to fulfil
cyflawniad accomplishment,
   achievement
cyflawniadau accomplishments,
   achievements
cyflawnir (is/will be) accomplished
cyflawnodd (he/she/it)
   accomplished

cyflawnwyd (was) accomplished
cyfle chance, opportunity
cyflenwad complement, supply
cyflenwadau supplies
cyflenwi to supply
cyflenwol complementary
cyflenwr supplier
cyflenwydd supplier
cyflenwyr suppliers
cyfleoedd opportunities
cyfleon opportunities
cyfleu to convey
cyfleus convenient, handy
cyfleuster convenience
cyfleusterau conveniences
cyfleustra convenience
cyflog pay, salary, wages
cyflogaeth employment
cyflogau wages
cyflogedig employed, salaried
cyflogeion employees
cyflogi to employ, to engage
cyflogwr employer
cyflogwyr employers
cyflogydd employer
cyflwr condition, state
cyflwyniad dedication,
   presentation
cyflwyniadau dedications,
   presentations
cyflwynir (is/will be) presented
cyflwyno to introduce, to
   present, to submit
cyflwynodd (he/she/it) presented
cyflwynwr presenter
cyflwynwyd (was) presented
cyflwynwyr presenters

cyflwynydd presenter
cyflym quick, rapid
cyflymach quicker
cyflymder speed, swiftness, velocity
cyflymdra speed
cyflymu to accelerate, to hasten
cyflyrau conditions
cyfnewid to exchange, to trade
cyfnewidiol changeable, variable
cyfnod era, period
cyfnodau periods, times
cyfnodol periodic
cyfnodolion periodicals
cyfnodolyn periodical
cyfochrog collateral, parallel
cyfoedion contemporaries
cyfoes contemporary
cyfoeth affluence, wealth
cyfoethog rich, wealthy
cyfoethogi to enrich, to make rich
cyfradd rate
cyfraddau rates
cyfraith law
cyfran share, portion, lot, quota
cyfranddaliadau shares
cyfraniad contribution
cyfraniadau contributions
cyfrannau shares
cyfrannodd (he/she/it) contributed
cyfrannol contributory
cyfrannu to contribute
cyfranogi to partake of, to participate
cyfranogiad participation

cyfranogwr participator
cyfranogwyr participators
cyfranwyr contributors
cyfredol concurrent, current
cyfreithiau laws
cyfreithiol judicial, legal
cyfreithiwr lawyer, solicitor
cyfreithlon lawful, legitimate
cyfreithwyr lawyers
cyfres list, serial, series
cyfresi series
cyfri to count
cyfrif[1] account
cyfrif[2] to calculate, to consider, to count
cyfrifeg accountancy
cyfrifiad calculation, census
cyfrifiadau censuses
cyfrifiadur computer
cyfrifiadurol computer
cyfrifiaduron computers
cyfrifir (is/will be) calculated
cyfrifo to calculate
cyfrifol responsible
cyfrifoldeb onus, responsibility
cyfrifoldebau responsibilities
cyfrifon accounts
cyfrinach secret
cyfrinachedd confidentiality
cyfrinachol confidential, secret
cyfrinair password
cyfrol volume
cyfrolau volumes
cyfrwng medium
cyfrwng-Cymraeg Welsh-medium
cyfryngau media

cyfryw such
cyfun comprehensive, united
cyfundeb union
cyfundrefn system
cyfundrefnau systems
cyfundrefnol systemic
cyfuniad blend, combination
cyfuniadau combinations
cyfuno to become one,
  to combine
cyfunol combined
cyfweld to interview
cyfweliad interview
cyfweliadau interviews
cyfwerth equal, equivalent
cyfyd (he/she/it) lifts
cyfyng[1] narrow, restricted
cyfyng[2] defile, gorge
cyfyngedig confined, limited
cyfyngiad limit
cyfyngiadau limits
cyfyngir (is/will be) restricted
cyfyngu to contract, to limit,
  to restrict
cyfystyr synonymous, tantamount
cyhoedd public
cyhoeddedig published
cyhoeddi to announce, to publish
cyhoeddiad announcement,
  publication
cyhoeddiadau announcements,
  publications
cyhoeddir (is/will be)
  announced, published
cyhoeddodd (he/she/it)
  announced, published
cyhoeddus public

cyhoeddusrwydd prominence,
  publicity
cyhoeddwr announcer, publisher
cyhoeddwyd (was) announced,
  published
cyhoeddwyr publishers
cyhuddiad accusation, charge
cyhuddiadau accusations
cyhuddo to accuse
cyhyd as long as, so long as
cyhyr muscle
cyhyrau muscles
cyhyryn muscle
cylch circle, group, hoop, orbit
cylchdaith circuit, orbit, tour
cylchdro rotation
cylched circuit
cylchgrawn journal, magazine,
  periodical
cylchgronau magazines
cylchlythyr circular, newsletter
cylchoedd circles
cylchrediad circulation
cyllell knife
cyllid income, revenue
cyllideb budget
cyllidebau budgets
cyllidir (is/will be) financed
cyllido to finance
cyllidol financial, fiscal
cyllyll knives
cymaint as many, as much,
  so much
cymal clause, joint
cymalau clauses, joints
Cymanwlad Commonwealth
cymar companion, mate, peer

cymariaethau comparisons
cymdeithas organisation, society
cymdeithasau societies
cymdeithasol sociable, social
cymdeithasu to socialise
cymdogaeth neighbourhood
cymdogion neighbours
cymedr arithmetic mean
cymedrig mean
cymedrol medium, moderate, temperate
cymell to incite, to urge
cymer[1] confluence
cymer[2] (you) take!
cymeradwy acceptable, approved
cymeradwyaeth applause, approval
cymeradwyir (is/will be) approved
cymeradwyo to applaud, to approve, to recommend
cymeradwywyd (was) approved
cymeriad character
cymeriadau characters
cymerir (is/will be) taken
cymerodd (he/she/it) took
cymerwch (you) take
cymerwyd (was) taken
cymesur symmetrical, proportionate
cymhareb ratio
cymhariaeth comparison, simile
cymharol comparative, moderate
cymharu to compare, to liken
cymharwch (you) compare

cymhelliad incentive, motive
cymhelliant motivation
cymhellion motives
cymhleth[1] complicated, elaborate
cymhleth[2] complex
cymhlethdod complexity
cymhorthdal grant, subsidy
cymhorthion aids
cymhwysedd competence
cymhwysiad adjustment, application
cymhwysir (is/will be) adapted
cymhwyso to adapt, to adjust
cymhwyster competence, suitability
cymoedd valleys
cymorth aid
cymorthdaliadau grants, subsidies
Cymraeg Welsh (language)
Cymraes Welshwoman
Cymreictod Welshness
Cymreig Welsh
Cymro Welshman
Cymru Wales
Cymry Welsh people
cymryd to take, to hold
cymun communion, Eucharist
cymuned community
cymunedau communities
cymunedol community
cymwys appropriate, direct, suitable
cymwysedig applied, qualified
cymwysiadau applications
cymwysterau qualifications

cymydog neighbour
cymylau clouds
cymysg mixed
cymysgedd concoction, mixture
cymysgu to confuse, to mix
cyn[1] before, previous to
cyn[2] as, so
cynadleddau conferences
cynaeafu to harvest
cynaladwyedd sustainability
cynaliadwy supportable, sustainable
cyndyn obstinate, reticent, stubborn
cynefin[1] accustomed, familiar
cynefin[2] habitat, haunt
cynefinoedd habitats
cynffon[1] appendage, tail
cynffon[2] tang, aftertaste
cyn-fyfyrwyr ex-students
cyngerdd concert
cynghanedd harmony, Welsh poetic alliteration
cyngherddau concerts
cynghorau councils
cynghori to advise, to counsel
cynghorir (is/will be) advised
cynghorwr adviser, councillor, counsellor
cynghorwyr councillors
cynghorydd councillor
cynghrair alliance, confederation, league
cyngor[1] advice, counsel
cyngor[2] council, senate
cynhadledd conference
cynhaeaf autumn, harvest

cynhaliaeth maintenance, support, upkeep
cynhaliodd (he/she/it) held
cynhaliol supporting
cynhaliwr supporter, upholder
cynhaliwyd (was) held
cynhalwyr supporters, upholders
cynhanesyddol prehistoric
cynharach earlier
cynharaf earliest
cynhelir (is/will be) held
cynhenid inherent, innate
cynhesu to warm
cynhwysedd capacity
cynhwysfawr capacious, comprehensive
cynhwysion ingredients
cynhwysir (is/will be) included
cynhwysol inclusive
cynhwyswyd (was) included
cynhwysydd container
cynhyrchiad production
cynhyrchiant production
cynhyrchiol productive, prolific
cynhyrchion ingredients
cynhyrchir (is/will be) produced
cynhyrchodd (he/she/it) produced
cynhyrchu to produce, to yield
cynhyrchwyd (was) produced
cynhyrchwyr producers
cynhyrchydd generator, producer
cyni hardship, straits
cynifer as many, so many
cynigiad motion, proposal
cynigion proposals

cynigir (is/will be) offered, proposed
cynigiwyd (was) offered, proposed
cynilion savings
cynilo to save
cynllun plan, plot, scheme
cynlluniau plans
cynllunio to design, to plan
cynlluniwyd (was) planned
cynnal to hold, to support, to sustain
cynnar early
cynnau to light, to switch on (the light)
cynnes affectionate, warm
cynnig[1] offer, proposal, try
cynnig[2] to offer, to propose, to try (for)
cynnil frugal, sparing, subtle
cynnwrf agitation, commotion
cynnwys[1] content, contents
cynnwys[2] to include, to contain, to consist
cynnydd growth, increase, progress
cynnyrch produce, product
cynorthwyo to assist, to help
cynorthwyol auxiliary, supporting
cynorthwywr assistant, helper
cynorthwywyr assistants
cynorthwyydd assistant
cynradd primary
cynrychiolaeth representation
cynrychioli to represent
cynrychiolir (is/will be) represented

cynrychiolwyr representatives
cynrychiolydd representative
cynt[1] quicker
cynt[2] before, formerly
cynta' first
cyntaf first, swiftest
cynted as soon as
cyntedd porch, vestibule
cyntefig primitive
cynulleidfa audience, congregation
cynulleidfaoedd audiences
cynulliad assembly, gathering
cynullydd convener
cynwysedig included, inclusive
cynyddodd (he/she/it) increased
cynyddol increasing, progressive
cynyddu to augment, to increase
cyraeddiadau attainments
cyrch attack
cyrchfan destination
cyrchu to make for
cyrff bodies
cyrhaeddiad attainment, comprehension, reach
cyrhaeddodd (he/she/it) reached
cyrion fringes
cyrn horns
cyrraedd to reach, to arrive, to attain
cyrsiau courses
cysegredig holy, sacred
cysgod reflection, shadow, shelter
cysgodion shadows
cysgodol shadow, shady, sheltered

cysgu to sleep
cyson consistent, constant, regular
cysondeb consistency, regularity
cysoni to reconcile
cystadlaethau competitions
cystadleuaeth competition
cystadleuol competitive
cystadleuwr competitor, rival
cystadleuwyr competitors
cystadlu to compete, to vie
cystal[1] as good as
cystal[2] equally, may as well
cysur comfort, consolation, solace
cysurus comfortable
cyswllt connection, link
cysyllta[1] (you) contact!, connect!
cysyllta[2] (he/she/it will) contact, connect
cysylltau contacts, links
cysyllter contact!, connect!
cysylltiad connection, contact, liaison
cysylltiadau contacts
cysylltiedig connected
cysylltiol associated, linked
cysylltir (is/will be) contacted, connected
cysylltu to connect, to join, to link

cysylltwch (you) contact, connect
cysyniad concept
cysyniadau concepts
cytbwys balanced, unbiased
cythraul demon, devil, fiend
cythreuliaid demons
cytsain consonance, consonant
cytseiniaid consonants
cytûn in agreement, of one mind
cytundeb agreement, contract, pact
cytundebau agreements, contracts
cytundebol contractual
cytunir (is/will be) agreed
cytuno to agree, to correspond
cytunodd (he/she/it) agreed
cytunwyd (was) agreed
cyw chick, nestling, youth, love, young animal
cywair key, register, tone
cywaith project
cywilydd disgrace, shame
cywion chicks
cywir correct, faithful, honest, true
cywirdeb accuracy, correctness
cywiro to correct
cywydd strict meter poem

D : d

a word starting with **d** printed in *italics* means that the root form
of that word begins with **t**, e.g. *dudalen* root **tudalen**
a word starting with **dd** printed in *italics* means that the root form
of that word begins with **d**, e.g. *ddafad* root *dafad*

in a Welsh dictionary, unlike this list, **dd** is a letter in its own right and
follows *dy* and precedes *e* alphabetically

da¹ good, well
da² cattle, goods, possessions
da³ pat, stroke
Dachwedd November
daclus tidy
dacw there, there (he, she, it) is,
   there (they) are
dad father
dadansoddi to analyse
dadansoddiad analysis, synopsis
dadansoddiadau analyses
dadansoddol analytical
dadau fathers
dad-cu grandfather
dadeni renaissance, revival
dadgofrestru to deregister
dadl argument, debate
dadlau to argue, to debate
dadlennu to disclose, to reveal
dadleth to thaw
dadleuol controversial,
   debatable
dadleuon arguments
dadlwytho to unload
dadlwythwch (you) unload
daear Earth, land, soil, lair
daeareg geology

daearegol geological
daearol earthly, terrestrial
daearyddiaeth geography
daearyddol geographical
daenu to spread
daer earnest, insistent
daeth (he/she/it) came, brought
daethant (they) brought, came
daethom (we) brought, came
daethpwyd (was) brought
dafad¹ sheep
dafad² wart
dafarn pub
daflen sheet
daflenni sheets
daflodd (he/she/it) threw
daflu to throw
dafod tongue
dafodiaith dialect
dagrau tears
dai houses
daid grandfather
dail¹ leaves
dail² dung, manure
daioni goodness
dair three
daith journey

dal¹ to catch, to capture, to hold, to maintain, to continue
dal² tall
dâl payment
daladwy payable
dalaith province, state
dalcen forehead
daleithiau provinces, states
dalen page, sheet
dalent talent
dalfa catch, gaol, prison
dalgylch catchment area
dalgylchoedd catchment areas
daliad¹ belief, opinion, catch
daliad² payment
daliadau¹ beliefs, convictions
daliadau² payments
daliodd (he/she/it) caught, held
dall blind, ignorant
dallt to understand
dalu to pay
dalwyd (was) paid
damaid bit
damcaniaeth hypothesis, theory
damcaniaethau hypotheses
damcaniaethol hypothetical, theoretical
damwain accident, mishap
damweiniau accidents
damweiniol accidental, inadvert
dan under
dân fire
danau fires
danfon to accompany, to send
dangos to demonstrate, to show
dangosir (is/will be) shown

dangosodd (he/she/it) showed
dangoswch (you) show
dangoswyd (was) shown
dangosydd indicator
dangosyddion indicators
dani under her
danio to fire, to ignite
dannedd teeth
dano under him
danseilio to undermine
dant¹ tooth
dant² string
danwydd fuel
danynt under them
danysgrifio to subscribe
dâp tape
darbwyllo to convince, to persuade
darddiad source
darfu¹ (he/she/it) ceased
darfu² to disturb, to interrupt, to scare
darganfod to discover
darganfuwyd (was) discovered
darganfyddiad discovery, find
darganfyddiadau discoveries
darged target
dargedau targets
dargedu to target
darlith lecture
darlithio to lecture
darlithoedd lectures
darlithwyr lecturers
darlithydd lecturer
darllediad broadcast
darllediadau broadcasts
darlledu to broadcast

darlledwr broadcaster
darllen to read
darllenadwy legible, readable
darlleniad reading
darlleniadau readings
darllenwch (you) read
darllenwr reader
darllenwyr readers
darllenydd reader
darlun illustration, picture,
   portrait
darluniau pictures
darlunio to draw, to illustrate,
   to portray
darn part, piece, portion
darnau pieces
daro[1] Oh dear!
daro[2] to hit, to strike
darogan to foretell, to predict
darostyngedig humble,
   subjugated
darpar designate, elect,
   prospective
darpariaeth preparation,
   provision
darpariaethau preparations
darparodd (he/she/it) prepared,
   provided
darparu to prepare, to provide
darparwr provider
darparwyd (was) prepared,
   provided
darparwyr providers
darparydd provider
darperir (is/will be) prepared,
   provided
darren knoll, rock

daru (he/she/it) did, happened
dasg task
dasgau tasks
data data
datblygedig developed
datblygiad development
datblygiadau developments
datblygir (is/will be) developed
datblygodd (he/she/it)
   developed
datblygu to develop
datblygwr developer
datblygwyd (was) developed
datblygwyr developers
datgan to announce, to declare,
   to proclaim
datganiad pronouncement,
   recital, statement
datganiadau announcements
datganodd (he/she/it)
   announced
datganoledig decentralised
datganoli to decentralise, to
   devolve
datgeliad disclosure
datgeliadau disclosures
datgelu to divulge, to reveal
datguddio to manifest, to reveal,
   to uncover
dathliad celebration
dathliadau celebrations
dathlu to celebrate
datrys to solve, to unravel,
   to untangle
datrysiad solution
datws potatoes
dau both, couple, two

daw¹ (he/she/it will) come
daw² silence
dawel quiet
dawelwch quiet
dawn flair, knack, talent
dawns dance
dawnsio to dance
dawnsiwr dancer
dawnswyr dancers
dawnus gifted, skilful
dda good
ddadansoddi to analyse
ddadansoddiad analysis
ddadl debate
ddadlau to argue, to debate
ddadleth to thaw
ddadleuon arguments
ddadlwytho to unload
ddaear Earth, land, soil, lair
ddaearyddiaeth geography
ddaearyddol geographical
ddaeth (he/she/it) brought,
    came
ddaethant (they) brought,
    came
ddafad sheep
ddagrau tears
ddail leaves
ddaioni goodness
ddal to catch, to hold
ddalen page, sheet
ddalfa catch, gaol, prison
ddaliad conviction, view
ddaliadau opinions, views
ddall blind
ddamcaniaeth theory
ddamwain accident

ddamweiniau accidents
ddamweiniol accidental
ddanfon to send
ddangos to show
ddangosir (is/will be) shown
ddangosodd (he/she/it) showed
ddangoswyd (was) shown
ddangosyddion indicators
ddannedd teeth
ddarfod to cease, to expire
ddarganfod to discover
ddarganfuwyd (was) discovered
ddarganfyddiadau discoveries
ddarlith lecture
ddarlithoedd lectures
ddarlithydd lecturer
ddarlledu to broadcast
ddarllen to read
ddarllenadwy legible
ddarllenwyr readers
ddarlun picture
ddarluniau pictures
ddarlunio to illustrate
ddarn part, piece, portion
ddarnau parts
ddarostyngedig subservient
ddarpar prospective
ddarpariaeth provision
ddarpariaethau preparations
ddarparu to prepare, to provide
ddarparwr provider
ddarparwyd (was) prepared,
    provided
ddarparwyr providers
ddarperir (is/will be) prepared,
    provided
ddaru (he/she/it) did, happened

ddata data
ddatblygiad development
ddatblygiadau developments
ddatblygir (is/will be) developed
ddatblygodd (he/she/it) developed
ddatblygu to develop
ddatblygwyd (was) developed
ddatgan to state
ddatganiad statement
ddatganiadau statements
ddatganoli to decentralise
ddatgelu to reveal
ddathlu to celebrate
ddatrys to solve
ddau two
ddaw (he/she/it) comes
ddawn ability
ddawns dance
ddawnsio to dance
dde right, south
ddeall to understand
ddealladwy intelligible
ddealltwriaeth understanding
ddeallus intelligent, wise
ddechrau to start
ddechreuodd (he/she/it) started
ddechreuwyd (was) started
ddeddf law
ddeddfau laws
ddeddfwriaeth legislation
ddedfryd sentence
ddedfrydu to sentence
ddedwydd happy
ddefaid sheep
ddeffro to wake
ddefnydd material, use

ddefnyddiau materials
ddefnyddid (would be/used to be) used
ddefnyddio to use
ddefnyddiodd (he/she/it) used
ddefnyddiol useful
ddefnyddir (is/will be) used
ddefnyddiwr user
ddefnyddiwyd (was) used
ddefnyddwyr users
ddeg ten
ddegawd decade
ddeheuol southerly
ddehongli to interpret
ddeialog dialogue
ddeilen leaf
ddeiliad holder, occupant
ddeiliaid holders, occupants
ddeillio to derive from
ddeilliodd (he/she/it) derived
ddeintyddion dentists
ddeintyddol dental
ddeiseb petition
ddelfrydol ideal
ddelio to deal
ddelir (is/will be) caught, held
ddelw idol, image
ddelwedd image
ddelweddau images
ddemocrataidd democratic
ddeng ten
ddengys (he/she/it) shows
ddeniadol attractive
ddenu to attract
dderbyn to accept
dderbyniadau receipts, receptions

dderbyniodd (he/she/it) accepted, received

dderbyniol acceptable

dderbyniwyd (was) accepted, received

dderbynnir (is/will be) accepted, received

dderwen oak tree

ddesg desk

ddethol select

ddetholiad selection

ddeuai (he/she/it would/used to) come

ddeuddeg twelve

ddeuddegfed twelfth

ddeugain forty

ddeunaw eighteen

ddeunawfed eighteenth

ddeunydd material

ddeunyddiau materials

ddewis[1] choice, selection

ddewis[2] to choose

ddewis[3] chosen, selected, optional

ddewisiadau choices

ddewisir (is/will be) chosen

ddewislen menu

ddewisodd (he/she/it) chose

ddewisol discretionary, select

ddewiswyd (was) chosen

ddewr brave

ddial revenge

ddiamau certain

ddiamod unconditional

ddianc to escape, to flee

ddiangen unnecessary

ddiau doubtless

ddiben purpose

ddibenion purposes

ddibwys unimportant

ddibynadwy dependable

ddibyniaeth dependency

ddibynnol dependent

ddibynnu to depend

ddichon perhaps

ddi-dâl unpaid

ddiddordeb interest

ddiddordebau interests

ddiddorol interesting

ddiddymu to annul, to repeal

ddi-dor unbroken

ddidrafferth effortless

ddiduedd objective, unbiased

ddidynnwyd (was) deducted, subtracted

ddieithr strange

ddieithriad without exception

ddifetha to spoil

ddiffiniad definition

ddiffinio to define

ddiffinnir (is/will be) defined

ddiffodd to extinguish, to put out

ddiffuant sincere

ddiffyg absence, lack

ddiffygiol lacking

ddiffygion defects

ddiflannu to disappear

ddiflas dull

ddifreintiedig underprivileged

ddifri serious

ddifrif serious

ddifrifol grave, serious

ddifrod damage

ddifrodi to destroy

ddifyr entertaining, interesting
ddig angry
ddigalon disheartened
ddigartref homeless
ddigidol digital
ddigon enough
ddigonol sufficient
ddigwydd to happen
ddigwyddiad event
ddigwyddiadau events
ddigwyddodd (he/she/it) happened
ddi-Gymraeg non-Welsh-speaking
ddileu to delete
ddillad clothes
ddilyn to follow
ddilyniant sequence
ddilynir (is/will be) followed
ddilynodd (he/she/it) followed
ddilynol following
ddilynwyr followers
ddilys authentic
ddilysu to authenticate
ddim not, nothing, zero
ddinas city
ddinasoedd cities
ddinasyddion citizens
ddinesig civic
ddinesydd citizen
ddinistrio to destroy
ddiniwed harmless
ddiod drink
ddioddef to suffer
ddioddefodd (he/she/it) suffered
ddioddefwyr sufferers, victims
ddiodydd drinks

ddiog lazy
ddiogel safe
ddiogelu to preserve, to protect
ddiogelwch safety
ddiolch[1] gratitude, thanks
ddiolch[2] to thank
ddiolchgar grateful
ddirfawr enormous
ddirgelwch[1] mystery
ddirgelwch[2] genitals
ddirprwy deputy
ddirprwyo to deputise
ddirwy fine
ddirwyn to wind up
ddirywiad decline
ddisg disc
ddisglair bright
ddisgrifiad description
ddisgrifiadau descriptions
ddisgrifio to describe
ddisgrifir (is/will be) described
ddisgrifiwyd (was) described
ddisgwyl to expect, to look
ddisgwyliadau expectations
ddisgwyliedig expected
ddisgwylir (is/will be) expected
ddisgybl pupil
ddisgyblaeth discipline
ddisgyblaethau disciplines
ddisgyblion pupils
ddisgyblu to discipline
ddisgyn to fall, to land
ddisodli to displace, to supplant
ddistaw quiet
ddiswyddiad dismissal
ddiswyddo to dismiss
ddi-waith unemployed

ddiwallu to satisfy
ddiwedd end
ddiweddar late, recent
ddiweddarach later
ddiweddaraf latest
ddiweddaru to update
ddiweithdra unemployment
ddiwethaf last
ddiwrnod day
ddiwrnodau days
ddiwyd diligent
ddiwydiannau industries
ddiwydiannol industrial
ddiwydiant industry
ddiwygiad revival (religious)
ddiwygiedig revised
ddiwygio to revise
ddiwylliannau cultures
ddiwylliannol cultural
ddiwylliant culture
ddiymdroi without delay
ddiystyru to ignore
ddod to come
ddodi to lay, to put
ddodrefn furniture
ddoe yesterday
ddoeth wise
ddoethineb wisdom
ddofn deep
ddogfen document
ddogfennaeth documentation
ddogfennau documents
ddogfennol documentary
ddolen link
ddoli doll
ddoniau skills
ddoniol amusing, funny

ddosbarth class, form
ddosbarthiad classification, distribution
ddosbarthiadau classes
ddosbarthu to distribute
ddosbarthwyd (was) distributed
ddosberthir (is/will be) distributed
ddraenen thorn
ddrafft draft, draught
ddraig dragon
ddrama dramas, play
ddramatig dramatic
ddringo to climb
ddrud costly, dear
ddrwg bad, wicked
ddrws door
ddrysau doors
ddryslyd muddled
ddryswch confusion
ddu black
ddull manner
ddulliau methods
ddur steel
dduw god
dduwiau gods
ddwbl double
ddweud to say
ddwfn deep
ddwfr water
ddŵr water
ddwy two
ddwyieithog bilingual
ddwylaw hands
ddwylo hands
ddwyn to steal
ddwyrain east
ddwyreiniol eastern

ddwys intense
ddwywaith twice
ddychmygu to imagine
ddychryn to frighten
ddychwelodd (he/she/it) returned
ddychwelyd to return
ddychymyg imagination
ddydd day
ddyddiad date
ddyddiadau dates
ddyddiau days
ddyddiol daily
ddyfais device
ddyfal diligent
ddyfalu to guess
ddyfarniad verdict
ddyfarnu to pronounce, to referee
ddyfarnwyd (was) refereed, adjudged, awarded
ddyfeisio to devise
ddyfernir (is/will be) refereed, adjudged, awarded
ddyffryn vale
ddyfnach deeper
ddyfnder depth
ddyfod to come
ddyfodiad arrival, newcomer
ddyfodol future
ddyfroedd waters
ddyfyniadau quotations
ddyfynnir (is/will be) quoted
ddyfynnu to quote
ddygwyd (was) brought, taken
ddylai (he/she/it) should
ddylanwad influence

ddylanwadau influences
ddylanwadu to influence
ddylech (you) should
ddyled debt
ddyledion debts
ddyledus indebted
ddylem (we) should
ddylen (they) should
ddylent (they) should
ddyletswydd duty
ddyletswyddau duties
ddylid (there) should
ddylunio to design
ddylwn (I) should
ddymchwel to overturn
ddymuniad desire
ddymuno to desire, to wish
ddymunol pleasant
ddyn man
ddynes woman
ddynion men
ddynodi to indicate
ddynodir (is/will be) denoted
ddynodwyd (was) denoted
ddynol human, manly, mortal
ddynoliaeth mankind
ddyrannu to allocate
ddysg learning
ddysgir (is/will be) learned, taught
ddysgl dish
ddysgodd (he/she/it) learned, taught
ddysgu to learn, to teach
ddysgwyd (was) learned, taught
ddysgwyr learners
ddywed (he/she/it) says
ddywedais (I) said

ddywedasant (they) said
ddywediad saying
ddywedir (is/will be) said
ddywedodd (he/she/it) said
ddywedwyd (was) said
ddywedyd to say
de[1] south
de[2] right
de[3] tea
deall[1] intellect, understanding
deall[2] to understand
dealladwy intelligible, understandable
deallol intellectual
dealltwriaeth agreement, understanding
deallus intelligent, wise
deallusol intellectual
deallusrwydd intelligence
debycach more like, more likely
debyd debit, debt
debyg[1] like, similar, likely
debyg[2] likelihood
debygol likely
decach fairer
dechneg technique
dechnegau techniques
dechnegol technical
dechnoleg technology
dechnolegau technologies
dechrau[1] beginning, start
dechrau[2] to begin, to start
dechreuad beginning
dechreuais (I) started
dechreuodd (he/she/it) started
dechreuol initial, original
dechreuwch (you) start

dechreuwyd (was) started
deddf act, law, statute
deddfau laws
deddfwriaeth legislation
deddfwriaethol legislative
de-ddwyrain south-east
dedfryd judgement, sentence, verdict
dedfrydau sentences
dedfrydu to sentence
dedwydd blessed, happy
defaid sheep
deffro to rouse, to wake
defnydd material, usage
defnyddiau materials
defnyddid (would be/used to be) used
defnyddio to use, to utilise
defnyddiodd (he/she/it) used
defnyddiol helpful, useful
defnyddir (is/will be) used
defnyddiwch (you) use
defnyddiwr consumer, user
defnyddiwyd (was) used
defnyddwyr consumers, users
defod ceremony, custom, rite
defodau customs, rites
deg[1] ten
deg[2] fair, fine
degau tens
degawd decade
degawdau decades
degwch beauty, fairness
degwm tithe
deheubarth south, southern part
deheuol southern

dehongli to interpret
dehongliad interpretation
dehongliadau interpretations
deialog dialogue
deiet diet
deigryn tear
deilen leaf
deiliad holder, occupant, tenant
deiliaid occupants
deillio to derive, to stem
deilliodd (he/she/it) derived
deillion blind (people)
deilwng deserving
deimlad feeling
deimladau feelings
deimlo to feel
deintydd dentist
deintyddion dentists
deintyddol dental
deipio to type
deirgwaith threefold, three times
deiseb petition
deithiau journeys
deithio to travel
deithiol peripatetic, travelling
deithwyr passengers, travellers
deitl title
deitlau titles
del pretty
deledu television
delerau terms
delfrydol ideal, idealistic
delio to deal
delir[1] (is/will be) caught, held
delir[2] (is/will be) paid
delta delta
delw effigy, idol, image, statue

delwedd image
delweddau images
delyn harp
deml temple
democrat democrat
democrataidd democratic
democratiaeth democracy
democratiaid democrats
demtasiwn temptation
denant tenant
denantiaeth tenancy
denantiaid tenants
denau thin
dendro to tender
deng ten
dengys (he/she/it) shows
deniadol alluring, attractive, inviting
denu to attract, to draw, to entice
deon dean
de-orllewin south-west
derbyn to accept, to admit, to receive
derbyniad reception
derbyniadau receipts
derbyniodd (he/she/it) accepted, received
derbyniol acceptable
derbyniwyd (was) accepted, received
derbynnir (is/will be) accepted, received
derbynnydd receiver, receptor
dere (you) come!
derfyn end
derfynau limits

derfynol final
derfynu to end, to terminate
deri oaks
derm term
dermau terms
derw oaks, oaken
derwen oak
'deryn bird
desg desk
destament testament
destun subject
destunau subjects
destunol textual, topical
dethol¹ choice, select
dethol² to choose, to select
detholiad selection
deuai (he/she/it would/used to) come
deuant (they/they will) come
deud to say, to tell
deuddeg twelve
deuddegfed twelfth
deuddeng twelve
deugain forty
deulawr two-storey
deulu family
deuluoedd families
deuluol domestic
deunaw eighteen
deunawfed eighteenth
deunydd content, material, matter, stuff, use
deunyddiau materials
deuocsid dioxide
deuol dual
deuwch (you) come!
dew fat

dewch (you) come!
dewis¹ choice, selection, the selected
dewis² to choose
dewis³ chosen, selected, optional
dewis⁴ (you) choose!
dewisiadau choices, options
dewisir (is/will be) chosen
dewislen menu
dewisodd (he/she/it) chose
dewisol choice, discretionary, select
dewiswch (you) choose
dewiswyd (was) chosen
dewr brave, valiant
dewrder bravery, courage, pluck
deyrnas kingdom
deyrnged tribute
di you
diafol demon, devil
diagnosis diagnosis
diagnostig diagnostic
diagram diagram
diagramau diagrams
dial¹ reprisal, revenge, vengeance
dial² to avenge
diamau certain, doubtless
diamod unconditional, unqualified
dianc to escape, to flee
diangen unnecessary
diau certain, sure, undoubted
diawl devil, bloody hell!
diben aim, purpose
dibenion aims
dibwys trivial, unimportant

dibynadwy dependable, reliable, trustworthy
dibynadwyedd dependability
dibyniaeth dependence, reliance
dibynnol dependent, subjunctive
dibynnu to depend, to rely upon
dichon perhaps
dichonoldeb feasibility, potentiality
dicter anger, wrath
di-dâl unpaid
diddanu to amuse, to console, to entertain
diddordeb interest
diddordebau interests
diddorol interesting
diddymu to abolish, to repeal
didoli to separate, to sort
di-dor incessant, unbroken, uninterrupted
didrafferth easy, trouble-free
diduedd impartial, unbiased
didynnu to deduct, to subtract
didynnwyd (was) deducted, subtracted
dieithr foreign, strange, uncommon
dieithriad without exception
difa to consume, to destroy, to ravage
difaru to regret
difaterwch apathy, indifference, nonchalance
diferu to drip, to trickle
difetha to destroy, to spoil
diffaith barren, desolate, paralysed, worthless

diffiniad definition
diffiniadau definitions
diffiniedig defined
diffinio to define
diffinnir (is/will be) defined
diffodd to extinguish, to go out, to put out, to turn off
diffuant genuine, sincere
diffyg defect, eclipse, shortfall
diffygiol defective, deficient, imperfect
diffygion shortcomings
diffynnydd defendant
diflannodd (he/she/it) disappeared
diflannu to disappear, to vanish
diflas boring, depressing, distasteful, dull
difreintiedig underprivileged
difri serious
difrif earnest, serious
difrifol earnest, grave, serious
difrifoldeb earnestness, seriousness
difrod damage, devastation
difrodi to destroy, to devastate
difyr agreeable, entertaining, pleasant
dig¹ anger, indignation
dig² angry, indignant, irate
digalon depressed, despondent, disheartened
digartref homeless
digido to digitise
digidol digital
digon¹ ample, enough, plenty
digon² enough, done, sufficient

digonedd abundance, plenty

digonol adequate, ample, sufficient

digwydd[1] to happen

digwydd[2] hardly

digwydd[3] action

digwyddiad event

digwyddiadau events

digwyddiadur event calendar

digwyddodd (he/she/it) happened

di-Gymraeg non-Welsh-speaking

diheintio to disinfect

dileu to abolish, to delete

dilëwyd (was) deleted

dillad bedclothes, clothes, garments

dilyn to follow, to pursue, to study, to succeed

dilyniant progression, sequence, sere

dilynir (is/will be) followed

dilynodd (he/she/it) followed

dilynol following, subsequent

dilynwch (you) follow!

dilynwr follower

dilynwyr followers

dilys authentic, genuine, valid

dilysrwydd genuineness, validity

dilysu to authenticate, to validate

dim any, anything, none, nothing, nought

dîm team

dimai halfpenny

dimau teams

dimensiwn dimension

din anus, bum

dinas city

dinasoedd cities

dinasyddiaeth citizenship

dinasyddion citizens

dinesig civic, municipal, urban

dinesydd citizen, inhabitant

dinistr destruction, havoc, ruin

dinistrio to annihilate, to destroy, to ruin

dinistriol destructive, ruinous

diniwed harmless, innocent, simple, unhurt, unscathed

diod drink, liquor

dioddef to endure, to suffer, to tolerate

dioddefaint suffering

dioddefodd (he/she/it) suffered

dioddefwr sufferer, victim

dioddefwyr sufferers

diodydd drinks

diog idle, lazy

diogel certain, safe, substantial

diogelir (is/will be) protected

diogelu to ensure, to preserve, to protect

diogelwch safety, security

diolch[1] gratitude, thanks

diolch[2] to thank

diolch[3] (you) thank!

diolchgar grateful, thankful

diolchodd (he/she/it) thanked

dip[1] dip

dip[2] tip

dipio to dip

diploma diploma

dipyn a bit

dir land
dirfawr enormous, immense
dirgel mysterious, secret
dirgelwch[1] mystery
dirgelwch[2] genitals
diriaethol concrete, tangible
diriogaeth territory
dirnad to comprehend, to
    fathom, to understand
diroedd lands
dirprwy deputy, surrogate
dirprwyedig deputised
dirprwyo to depute, to deputise
    for
dirwedd landscape, relief
dirwy fine
dirwyn to coil, to wind up
dirwyon fines
dirymu to annul, to revoke
dirywiad decline, degeneration,
    deterioration
dirywio to degrade, to
    deteriorate
disg disc
disglair bright, brilliant, dazzling
disgleirio to shine, to sparkle
disgownt discount
disgresiwn discretion
disgrifiad description
disgrifiadau descriptions
disgrifio to describe
disgrifiodd (he/she/it) described
disgrifir (is/will be) described
disgrifiwch (you) describe
disgrifiwyd (was) described
disgwyl to await, to expect,
    to look

disgwyliad expectation
disgwyliadau expectations
disgwylid (used to be) expected
disgwyliedig anticipated,
    expected
disgwylir (is/will be) expected
disgwyliwn (we/we will) expect
disgybl disciple, pupil
disgyblaeth discipline
disgyblaethau disciplines
disgyblion pupils
disgyblu to discipline
disgyn to dismount, to fall, to land
disgyrchiant gravity
disodli to displace, to supplant
distaw calm, peaceful, quiet,
    silent, soft
distawrwydd silence, stillness
diswyddiad dismissal, sack
diswyddo to dismiss, to sack
dithau yourself
di-waith redundant, unemployed
diwallu to satisfy
diwedd close, end
diweddar late, recent
diweddara latest
diweddarach later
diweddaraf latest
diweddariad revision, update
diweddaru to modernise,
    to update
diweddarwyd (was) updated
diweddglo conclusion, finale
diweddu to end, to finish
diweithdra unemployment
diwethaf last
diwinyddiaeth theology

diwinyddol theological
diwrnod day
diwrnodau days
diwtoriaid tutors
diwyd assiduous, diligent
diwydiannau industries
diwydiannol industrial
diwydiant industry
diwyg appearance, format
diwygiad reform, revival
diwygiadau reforms, revivals
  (religious)
diwygiedig amended, revised
diwygio to amend, to reform,
  to revise
diwygiwyd (was) amended,
  reformed
diwylliannau cultures
diwylliannol cultural
diwylliant culture
diymdroi immediate, without
  delay
diystyru to disregard, to ignore
dlawd poor
dlodi poverty
dlos pretty
do[1] yes
do[2] doh
do[3] roof
do[4] generation
doc[1] dock
doc[2] slice
doctor doctor
docyn[1] tag, ticket, token
docyn[2] slice, packed lunch
docynnau tickets, tokens
dod to come, to bring, to become

dodi to plant, to put
dodrefn furniture
dodwy to lay
doe yesterday
doedd (he/she/it/there) wasn't
doeddwn (I) wasn't
does[1] (there) isn't
does[2] dough, pastry
doeth discreet, wise
doethineb sagacity, wisdom
dofednod poultry
dofn deep
dogfen document
dogfennaeth documentation
dogfennau documents
dogfennol documentary
doi (you/you will) come
dôl[1] dale, meadow
dôl[2] dole
dolen handle, link, loop
dolennau handles, links, loops
dolenni links
doli doll
Dolig Christmas
doll tax, toll
dolur anguish, hurt, wound
dolydd meadows
dom manure
domen dump, dunghill
domestig domestic
don wave
dôn tune
doniau abilities, gifts
doniol amusing, humorous
donnau waves
dop top
dor belly, midriff

dorf crowd
doriad break, cut
dorri to break
dorrodd (he/she/it) broke, cut
dos[1] (you) go!
dos[2] dose
dosbarth class, division, form
dosbarthiad classification, distribution
dosbarthiadau classes
dosbarthu to arrange, to classify, to distribute
dosbarthwyd (was) distributed
dosberthir (is/will be) distributed
dost[1] ill, sore, unwell
dost[2] toast
dowch (you) come!
down (we/we will) come
Dr doctor
dra extremely, very
drachefn again
draddodi to commit, to deliver
draddodiad tradition
draddodiadau traditions
draddodiadol traditional
draean a third
draed feet
draenen thorn-tree
draeniad drainage
draenio to drain
draenog hedgehog
draeth beach
draethau beaches
draethawd dissertation, essay
drafferth difficulty
drafferthion difficulties

draffig traffic
drafft[1] draft
drafft[2] draught
drafftio to draft
drafnidiaeth traffic
drafod to discuss
drafodaeth discussion
drafodaethau discussions
drafodion proceedings, transactions
drafodir (is/will be) discussed
drafodwyd (was) discussed
dragwyddol eternal
dragywydd eternal
draig dragon
drain thorns
drais rape, violence
drama dramas, play
dramatig dramatic
dramâu dramas, plays
dramgwydd hindrance
dramodwr dramatist, playwright
dramodydd dramatist, playwright
dramor overseas
drannoeth next day
dras kin, pedigree
draul wear
draw[1] there, yonder
draw[2] pitch (sound)
drawiadol striking
draws across, cross
drawsnewid to transform
dre town
drech superior
drechu to defeat
dref town

drefi towns
drefn order
drefniadaeth organisation
drefniadau arrangements
drefniant arrangement
drefnir (is/will be) arranged, organised
drefnu to arrange
drefnus orderly
drefnwyd (was) arranged, organised
drefol urban
dreftadaeth heritage
dreigiau dragons
dreigl passage
drenau trains
dreth tax
drethadwy taxable
drethi rates, taxes
drethu to tax
dreuliau expenses
dreulio to spend
dreuliodd (he/she/it) spent
dri three
dribiwnlys tribunal
drigolion inhabitants
drin to treat
drindod trinity
dringo to climb, to scale
driniaeth treatment
driniaethau treatments
drio to try
drist sad
dristwch sadness
dro[1] turn, bend, change
dro[2] journey, walk
dro[3] time

drodd (he/she/it) turned
droed foot
droedfeddi feet (distance)
droeon[1] turns, bends, changes
droeon[2] times
droi to turn, to twist, to stir, to dig, to upset, to change
drol cart
drom heavy
dros for, over
drosedd crime
droseddau crimes
droseddol criminal
droseddu to commit an offence
droseddwyr criminals, culprits
drosglwyddiad transference
drosglwyddir (is/will be) transferred
drosglwyddo to transfer
drosglwyddwyd (was) transferred
drosi to convert, to translate
drosoch for you, over you
drosodd for, over
drosom for us, over us
drosti for her, over her
drosto for him, over him
drostynt for them, over them
drot trot
drothwy threshold
drowyd (was) turned
druan poor thing
drud costly, dear, valuable
drueni pity
druenus piteous
drugaredd mercy
drugarog merciful

drwch thickness
drwchus thick
drwg[1] evil, harm
drwg[2] bad, evil, naughty, rotten
drwm heavy
drwodd through
drws door, doorway, gap
drwsio to mend
drwy as, because, by means of, through
    drwy'i because of his/her/its, by means of his/her/its, through his/her/its
drwyadl thorough
drwydded licence
drwyddedau licences
drwyddedu to licence
drwyddi through her/it
drwyddo through him/it
drwyddynt through them
drwyn nose
drych image, looking-glass, mirror
drychineb disaster
drydan electricity
drydedd third (feminine)
drydydd third (masculine)
drygioni evil, mischief, wickedness
dryloyw transparent
drylwyr thorough
drysau doors
dryslyd confused, muddled, tangled
drysor treasure
drysorau treasures
drysu to be confused, to bewilder, to entangle, to mess up
dryswch bewilderment, confusion
drywydd track
du[1] black, dark, dirty
du[2] side
dudalen page
dudalennau pages
duedd tendency
dueddiadau tendencies
dueddol inclined, liable
dug duke
dull manner, method, style
dulliau methods
duon black
dur[1] steel
dur[2] hard, steel
duw god
duwiau gods
duwiol devout, godly, pious
dwad to come
dŵad to come
dwbercwlosis tuberculosis
dwbl double
dweud to assert, to claim, to say, to tell
dwf growth
dwfn deep, profound
dwfr water
dwll hole
dwp silly
dwr crowd, heap
dŵr[1] water
dŵr[2] tower
dwristiaeth tourism
dwristiaid tourists
dwsin dozen

dwt neat, tidy
dwy two
dwyfol divine, sacred
dwyieithog bilingual
dwyieithrwydd bilingualism
dwylaw hands
dwyll deceit
dwyllo to deceive
dwylo hands
dwyn[1] to bear, to steal
dwyn[2] dune, knoll
dwyrain east
dwyreiniol easterly, eastern, oriental
dwys concentrated, intense, profound, serious
dwysedd density
dwyt (you) are not
dwywaith double, twice
dy thine, thy, you, your
dybiaeth presumption
dybio to presume
dyblu to double, to repeat
dyblygu to duplicate
dybryd atrocious, dire, monstrous
dychmygol fictitious, imaginary, imaginative
dychmygu to fancy, to imagine, to picture
dychmygus imaginative, inventive
dychmygwch (you) imagine
dychryn[1] fright, scare, terror
dychryn[2] to be frightened, to frighten, to terrify
dychrynllyd[1] awful, dreadful, terrible
dychrynllyd[2] awfully, terribly, very

dychwelodd (he/she/it) returned
dychwelwch (you) return
dychwelyd to return, to revert
dychymyg fancy, imagination, riddle
dydd day
dyddiad date
dyddiadau dates
dyddiadur diary
dyddiaduron diaries
dyddiau days
dyddiedig dated
dyddio to date, to dawn
dyddiol daily
dyddlyfr diary
dydi (he/she/it) isn't
dydw (I) am not
dydy (he/she/it) isn't
dydych (you) are not
dydyn (we/they) are not
dyfais device, invention, stratagem
dyfal diligent, painstaking, persistent
dyfalu to guess, to work out
dyfarniad adjudication, verdict
dyfarniadau verdicts
dyfarnu to referee, to adjudicate, to umpire, to award, to pronounce, to give a verdict
dyfarnwr referee, umpire
dyfarnwyd (was) refereed, adjudged, awarded
dyfeisgar ingenious, inventive, resourceful
dyfeisiau devices

dyfeisio to devise, to invent
dyfernir (is/will be) refereed, adjudged, awarded
dyffryn vale, valley
dyffrynnoedd vales, valleys
dyfi (you) grow
dyfiant growth
dyfnach deeper
dyfnder depth, intensity, profundity
dyfnion deep
dyfod to come
dyfodiad arrival, newcomer
dyfodol future
dyfrgi otter
dyfrgwn otters
dyfrhau to irrigate, to water
dyfroedd waters
dyfu to grow
dyfyniad extract, quotation
dyfyniadau quotations
dyfynnir (is/will be) quoted
dyfynnu to cite, to quote
dygwyd (was) brought, taken
dygymod to accept, to come to terms with
dyhead aspiration, longing, yearning
dyheadau aspirations
dyheu to aspire, to long for, to yearn
dylai (he/she/it) should
dylanwad influence
dylanwadau influences
dylanwadol influential
dylanwadu to hold sway, to influence
dylech (you) should

dyled debt
dyledion debts
dyledus due, indebted, outstanding
dyledwr debtor
dyledwyr debtors
dylem (we) should
dylen (they) should
dylent (they) should
dyletswydd devotion, duty
dyletswyddau duties
dylid (there) should
dyllau holes
dyluniad design
dyluniadau designs
dylunio to design
dyluniwyd (was) designed
dylwn (I) should
dyma here is, these are, this is
dymchwel to demolish, to overthrow, to overturn
dymheredd temperature
dymhorol seasonal
dymor season, term
dymunant (they) wish
dymuniad desire, wish
dymuniadau desires, wishes
dymuno to desire, to like, to wish
dymunol agreeable, delightful, pleasant
dymunwch (you) wish
dymunwn (we/we will) wish
dyn man, mortal
dyna that is, there is, those are
dyner tender
dynes female, woman
dyngarol humane, humanitarian, philanthropic

dynged fate
dyngedfennol crucial, fateful
dyniaethau humanities
dynion men
dynn tight
dynnir[1] (is/will be) pulled,
　subtracted, removed
dynnir[2] (is/will be) drawn,
　photographed
dynnodd[1] (he/she/it) pulled,
　subtracted, removed
dynnodd[2] (he/she/it) drew,
　photographed
dynnu[1] to pull, to subtract,
　to remove
dynnu[2] to draw, to photograph
dynnwyd[1] (was) pulled,
　subtracted, removed
dynnwyd[2] (was) drawn,
　photographed
dynodedig designated
dynodi to denote, to indicate
dynodir (is/will be) denoted
dynodwyd (was) denoted
dynol human, manly, mortal
dynoliaeth humaneness,
　humanity, mankind
dynwared to copy, to imitate,
　to mimic
dyraniad allocation
dyraniadau allocations
dyrannu to allocate, to dissect,
　to share out
dyrchafiad preferment, promotion
dyrchafu to elevate, to lift,
　to promote
dyrfa crowd

dyrys complicated, entangled,
　intricate, perplexing
dysg learning
dysgeidiaeth doctrine, teaching
dysgir (is/will be) learned, taught
dysgl dish, platter
dysgodd (he/she/it) learned,
　taught
dysgu to learn, to memorise,
　to teach
dysgwr learner
dysgwyd (was) learned, taught
dysgwyr learners
dyst witness
dystiolaeth evidence
dystion witnesses
dystysgrif certificate
dystysgrifau certificates
dyw (he/she/it) isn't
dywed (he/she/it) says
dywedai (he/she/it would/
　used to) say
dywedais (I) said
dywedasant (they) said
dyweder let's say, (were it) said
dywediad saying
dywedir (is/will be) said
dywedodd (he/she/it) said
dywedwch (you) let's say, say
dywedwyd (was) said
dywedyd to say
dywod sand
dywydd weather
dywyll dark
dywysoges princess
dywysogion princes

E : e

a word starting with **e** printed in *italics* means that the root form of that word begins with **g**, e.g. *eiriau* root **geiriau**

e he, him, it
eang broad, extensive, wide
ebe (he/she/it) said
e-bost electronic mail, e-mail
e-bostia (you) e-mail
e-bostio to e-mail
e-bostiwch (you) e-mail
ebr (he/she/it) said
Ebrill April
echdyniad extraction
echdyniadau extractions
echdynnu to extract
echdynwyr extractors
ecoleg ecology
ecolegol ecological
economaidd economic
economeg economics
economi economy
ecosystem ecosystem
ecosystemau ecosystems
edau cotton, thread, yarn
e-ddysgu e-learning
edmygedd admiration
edmygu to admire, to esteem
edrych[1] to look
edrych[2] (you) look!
edrychai (he/she/it would/ used to) look
edrychodd (he/she/it) looked
edrychwch (you) look!
edrychwn (we/we will) look

ef he, him, it
efail smithy
efallai maybe, perhaps, possibly
e-fasnach e-commerce
efe he, him
efelychu to emulate, to imitate
efengyl Gospel, gospel truth
efengylaidd evangelical
effaith effect
effeithiau effects
effeithio to affect, to effect
effeithiodd (he/she/it) affected, effected
effeithiol effective, efficient
effeithiolrwydd effectiveness, efficacy
effeithir (is/will be) affected, effected
effeithiwyd (was) affected, effected
effeithlon efficient
effeithlonrwydd efficiency
effro alert, awake, vigilant
efo together with, with
    efo'i with his/her/its
e-fusnes e-business
efydd[1] brass, bronze
efydd[2] brassy
e-gardiau e-cards
egin shoots
eglur clear, distinct, plain

eglurdeb clarity, clearness
eglurder clarity
eglurhad explanation
egluro to clarify, to enlighten, to explain
eglurodd (he/she/it) explained
eglurwch (you) explain
eglwys church, the Church
eglwysi churches
eglwysig ecclesiastical
egni energy, might
egnïol energetic, strenuous, vigorous
egwyddor principle, rudiments
egwyddorion principles
egwyl break, intermission, interval
ehangach wider
ehangaf widest
ehangder breadth, expanse, stretch
ehangiad extension
ehangu to broaden, to expand
ehebiaeth email
ei¹ her, him, his, its
ei² (you/you will) go
eich your
eicon icon
Eidal Italy
Eidalaidd Italian
Eidaleg Italian (language)
eiddgar ardent, enthusiastic, zealous
eiddo¹ belongings, possessions, property
eiddo² belong
eidion bullock

Eifftiad Egyptian
Eifftiaid Egyptians
eigion bottom, depths, the deep
eilaidd secondary
eiliad moment, second
eiliadau seconds
eilradd secondary, second-rate
eilwaith again, second time
ein our, us
Eingl Angles
einioes life, lifetime
eir (will) go
eira snow
eirfa vocabulary
eiriau words
eirin plums
eiriolaeth advocacy, intercession
eironig ironic
eisiau want, need, lack, destitution
eisio to ice
eisoes already
eistedd¹ to lie, to seat, to sit
eistedd² sitting
eisteddai (he/she/it would/ used to) sit
eisteddfod competitive meeting
eisteddfodau competitive meetings
eisteddfodol of/like an eisteddfod
eisteddodd (he/she/it) sat
eitem item
eitemau items
eithaf¹ quite
eithaf² extreme, ultimate, limit, extremity

eithafol excessive, extreme
eithin furze, gorse, whin
eithr but, save that
eithriad exception
eithriadau exceptions
eithriadol exceptional,
  outstanding
eithriedig excepted, excluded,
  exempt
eithrio to except, to exclude,
  to exempt
electroneg electronics
electronig electronic
eleni this year
elfen aptitude, element, factor
elfennau elements
elfennol elementary, rudimentary
eli balm, ointment
eliffant elephant
elifiant effluence
elli (you) are able, can
ellid (would/used to) be able
ellir (is/will be) able
ellwch (you) are able, can
elusen alms, charity
elusennau charities
elusennol charitable
elw gain, proceeds, profit
elwa to benefit, to profit
elwid (would be/used to be)
  called
elwir (is/will be) called
elyn enemy
elynion enemies
em gem
emosiwn emotion
emosiynau emotions

emosiynol emotional
emyn hymn
emynau hymns
enaid soul
enau mouth
enbyd grievous, perilous
endid entity
enedigaeth birth
enedigol native
eneidiau souls
eneth girl
enetig genetic
enfawr colossal, enormous,
  immense
enghraifft example
enghreifftiau examples
enghreifftiol illustrative
englyn verse
englynion verses
eni to be born
enillion earnings, spoils, winnings
enillir (is/will be) won
enillodd (he/she/it) won
enillwr winner
enillwyd (was) won
enillwyr winners
enillydd winner
ennill to earn, to gain, to obtain,
  to win
ennyd while
ennyn to awaken, to ignite,
  to kindle
entrepreneur entrepreneur
entrepreneuraidd
  entrepreneurial
entrepreneuriaeth
  entrepreneurship

entrepreneuriaid
  entrepreneurs
enw name, noun, reputation
enwad denomination
enwadau denominations
enwau names, nouns
enwebedig nominated
enwebiad nomination
enwebiadau nominations
enwebu to nominate
enwebwyd (was) nominated
enwedig especially, particularly
enwi to call, to name
enwir (is/will be) named
enwocaf most famous
enwog celebrated, famous, noted
enwogion celebrities
enwogrwydd fame, renown
enwyd (was) named
eog salmon
eogiaid salmon (plural)
epistol epistle
er despite, since
eraill others
erbyn[1] after, by, by the time, in time for
erbyn[2] against, versus
erchyll dreadful, hideous, horrible
erfyn[1] instrument, tool
erfyn[2] to beg, to crave, to entreat, to expect, to implore, to supplicate
ergyd aim, blast, blow, shot
erioed ever, never, (not) at all
erledigaeth persecution
erlid to hound, to persecute

erlyn to prosecute, to sue
erlyniad prosecution
ers since
erthygl article, clause
erthyglau articles
erw acre
erwau acres
erydiad erosion
erydu to erode
eryr[1] eagle
eryr[2] herpes, shingles
erys (he/she/it) stays
es (I) went
esblygiad evolution
esblygu to evolve
esboniad commentary, explanation
esboniadau commentaries, explanations
esboniadol explanatory
esbonio to explain
esboniodd (he/she/it) explained
esboniwch (you) explain
esgeuluso to disregard, to neglect, to shirk
esgeulustod carelessness, negligence
esgid boot, shoe
esgidiau shoes
esgob bishop
esgobaeth bishopric, diocese
esgobion bishops
esgor to give birth to
esgus[1] excuse, pretext
esgus[2] feign, pretend to
esgyn to ascend, to mount, to rise

esgyrn bones
esiampl example
esiamplau examples
esmwyth easy, glib, smooth
esthetaidd aesthetic
esthetig aesthetic
estron[1] alien, foreign
estron[2] alien, foreigner
estyn to extend, to hand,
    to stretch
estynedig extended
estyniad extension
estyniadau extensions
estynnodd (he/she/it) handed,
    reached
ethnig ethnic
ethol to elect
etholaeth constituency,
    electorate, ward
etholaethau constituencies
etholedig elect
etholiad election
etholiadau elections
etholiadol electoral
etholwr constituent, elector,
    voter

etholwyd (was) elected
etholwyr electors
ethos ethos
etifedd heir, inheritor
etifeddiaeth inheritance
etifeddu to inherit
eto[1] still, yet
eto[2] again, ditto
eu their, them
euog guilty
euogfarn conviction
euogfarnau convictions
euogrwydd guilt
euraid golden
euraidd golden
euthum (I) went
ewch (you) go
ewro euro
Ewrop Europe
Ewropeaidd European
ewyllys will
ewyn foam, froth, scum
ewythr uncle

F : f

a word starting with **f** printed in *italics* means that the root form
of that word begins with **b**, e.g. *fabanod* root **babanod;**
or with **m**, e.g. *fab* root **mab**

in a Welsh dictionary, unlike this list, **ff** is a letter in its own right and
follows *fy* and precedes *g* alphabetically

fab son
fabanod babies
fabwysiadu to adopt
fabwysiadwyd (was) adopted
fach little, small
fachgen boy
fae bay
faen stone
faenor manor
faer mayor
faes field
faethu to nurture
fag bag
fagu to nurse, to rear
fagwyd (was) nursed, reared
fai fault
Fai may
faich burden
fain narrow, slim
fainc bench
faint[1] how many?, how much?
faint[2] much, size
faith long
'falau apples
falch glad, proud
falchder pride
falu to grind

falle perhaps
fam mother
famau mothers
fam-gu grandmother
fan[1] van
fan[2] mark, place, spot
fân small, tiny
fanc bank
fanciau banks
fand band
fandaliaeth vandalism
fandiau bands
faner flag
fangre place, premises
fannau[1] places
fannau[2] peaks
fantais advantage
fanteisio to take advantage
fanteisiol advantageous
fanteision advantages
fantell cloak
fantol balance
fantolen balance sheet
fanwl detailed
fanylach more detailed
fanylder detail
fanyleb specification

fanylebau specifications
fanylion details
fap map
fapiau maps
fapio to map
far bar
fara bread
farc mark
farchnad market
farchnadoedd markets
farchnata to market, to trade
farciau marks
farcio to mark
fardd bard, poet
farddoniaeth poetry
fargen bargain
farn nuisance, opinion
farnau opinions
farnu to judge
farnwr judge
farnwriaeth judiciary
farw dead, die
farwolaeth death
farwolaethau deaths
fas[1] shallow
fas[2] bass
fas[3] out
fasged basket
fasnach trade
fasnachol commercial
fasnachu to trade
fasnachwyr traders
faswn (I) would have
fater matter
faterion matters
fath[1] such
fath[2] kind, sort, type

fàth bath
fathau sorts
fawr big
Fawrth[1] March
Fawrth[2] Tuesday
Fawrth[3] Mars
fe[1] {*introduces a statement*}
   fe'ch you
   fe'i he, him, it, she
   fe'u they
fe[2] he, him, it
fecanyddol mechanical
fechan little
fechgyn boys
fedal medal
fedd[1] grave
fedd[2] mead
feddal soft
feddalwedd software
feddiannu to possess
feddiannydd occupant, owner
feddiant possession
feddu to possess
feddwl[1] to think
feddwl[2] mind
feddyg doctor
feddygfa surgery
feddyginiaeth cure, treatment
feddygol medical
feddygon doctors
feddyliau thoughts
feddyliol mental
Fedi September
fedr ability
fedrai (he/she/it would/used to)
   be able
fedrau skills

fedru to be able
fedrus capable
fedrwch (you) are able, can
fedrwn (we are/will be) able
Fehefin June
feibion sons
feic bike
feichiog pregnant
feini slabs, stones
feirdd bards, poets
feirniadaeth criticism
feirniadol critical
feirniadu to adjudge, to adjudicate, to criticise
feirniaid adjudicators, critics
feistr master
feithrin to nurture
feithrinfa nursery
fel as, how, like, similar
fêl honey
felen yellow
felin mill
felly so, such, therefore
felyn yellow
felys sweet
fendigedig excellent, great
fendith blessing
fenter venture
fenthyca to borrow, to lend
fenthyciad loan
fenthyciadau loans
fenthyg[1] to borrow
fenthyg[2] borrowed
fentrau ventures
fentro to dare, to venture
fenyw woman
fenywod women

fer short
ferch girl
ferched girls
Fercher[1] Wednesday
Fercher[2] Mercury
ferf verb
fersiwn version
fersiynau versions
fertigol vertical
ferwi to boil
festri vestry
fesul by
fesur to measure
fesurau measurements
fetel metal
fethiannau failures
fethiant failure
fethodd (he/she/it) failed
fethodoleg methodology
fethu to fail
fetrig metric
feunyddiol daily
fewn in
fewnforio to import
fewnfudwyr immigrants
fewnol internal
feysydd fields
ffa[1] beans, broad beans
ffa[2] fah
ffacs fax (facsimile)
ffactor factor
ffactorau factors
ffafr favour
ffafrio to favour, to prefer
ffafriol favourable, preferential
ffair fair, market
ffaith fact

ffanatig fanatic
ffansi fancy
ffarm farm
ffarmwr farmer
ffarwelio to bid farewell
ffasiwn[1] fashion, vogue
ffasiwn[2] sort, such
ffasiynol fashionable
ffatri factory
ffatrïoedd factories
ffawd destiny, fate, fortune
ffederal federal
ffederasiwn federation
ffefryn favourite, pet
ffefrynnau favourites
ffeil file
ffeiliau files
ffeilio to file
ffeindio to find
ffeiriau fairs
ffeithiau facts
ffeithiol factual, non-fiction
ffenest window
ffenestr window
ffenestri windows
ffens fence
ffensys fences
fferi ferry
fferm farm
ffermdai farmhouses
ffermdy farmhouse
ffermio to farm
ffermwr farmer
ffermwyr farmers
ffermydd farms
fferyllol pharmaceutical
fferyllwyr pharmacists

fferyllydd chemist, pharmacist
ffi fee
ffibr fibre, roughage
ffidil fiddle, violin
ffidl fiddle, violin
ffigur figure
ffigwr figure
ffigyrau figures
ffilm film, movie
ffilmiau films
ffilmio to film
ffin border, boundary, frontier
ffiniau borders
ffioedd fees
ffiseg physics
ffisegol physical
ffit fit
ffitio to fit
ffitrwydd fitness, suitability
fflach flash, glint, match
fflam flame
fflamau flames
fflat flat
fflatiau flats
ffliw[1] flu, influenza
ffliw[2] flue
fflur flowers
fflyd crowd, fleet, gang
ffo escape, flight
ffoadur fugitive, refugee
ffoaduriaid refugees
ffocws focus
ffocysu to focus
ffodus fortunate, lucky
ffoi to flee, to run away
ffolder folder
ffolineb folly, foolishness, silliness

ffon stick, walking-stick, rung
ffôn phone, telephone
ffonau telephones
ffonio to phone, to telephone
ffoniwch (you) phone
ffont font, fount
ffordd road, route, way
fforddiadwy affordable
fforddio to afford
fforest forest
fforestydd forests
fformat format
fformatau formats
fformiwla formula
fformiwlâu formulae
ffortiwn fortune
fforwm forum
fforymau fora, forums
ffos ditch, moat, trench
ffosydd ditches, trenches
ffotograff photograph
ffotograffaidd photographic
ffotograffau photographs
ffotograffiaeth photography
ffotograffig photographic
ffotograffydd photographer
ffrae quarrel, squabble
ffraeo to quarrel, to squabble
ffraeth facetious, witty
ffrâm frame
fframiau frames
fframwaith framework, structure
fframweithiau structures
fframyn frame
Ffrangeg French (language)
Ffrengig French

ffres fresh
ffrind friend
ffrindiau friends
ffrio to fry
ffroen muzzle, nostril
ffroenau nostrils
ffrog dress, frock
ffrwd brook, stream
ffrwydro to blast, to explode
ffrwydron explosives
ffrwydryn detonator, explosive
ffrwyth[1] fruit, berry
ffrwyth[2] product, result
ffrwythau[1] fruits, berries
ffrwythau[2] products, results
ffrwythlon fertile, fruitful, lush
ffrwythyn piece of fruit
ffrydiau streams
ffrynt front
ffug counterfeit, fake, false
ffuglen fiction
ffurf form, shape
ffurfafen firmament
ffurfiau forms
ffurfio to form
ffurfiol formal
ffurfiwyd (was) formed
ffurflen form, pro forma
ffurflenni forms
ffwng fungus
ffwrdd away
ffwrn oven
ffwrnais furnace
ffydd confidence, faith
ffyddiog confident
ffyddlon faithful, loyal, true
ffyddlondeb faithfulness, fidelity

ffyn sticks
ffynhonnau fountains, springs
ffynhonnell fount, source, spring
ffyniannus prosperous, successful
ffyniant prosperity, success
ffynnon fount, spring, well
ffynnu to prosper, to succeed, to thrive
ffynonellau sources, wells
ffyrdd ways
ffyrnig ferocious, fierce
fi I, me
ficer[1] vicar
ficer[2] beaker
Fictoraidd Victorian
fideo video
fideos videos
fil[1] bill
fil[2] thousand
filiwn million
filiynau millions
filltir mile
filltiroedd miles
filoedd thousands
filwr soldier
filwrol military
filwyr soldiers
fin[1] bin
fin[2] edge, point, verge
finnau myself
fioamrywiaeth biodiversity
firws virus
firysau viruses
fis month
fisoedd months
fisol monthly
fitamin vitamin

fitaminau vitamins
fiwsig music
flaen front, point, tip
flaenaf foremost
flaenddalen title page
flaengar prominent
flaenllaw foremost
flaenoriaeth priority
flaenoriaethau priorities
flaenoriaethu to prioritise
flaenorol previous
flas taste
flasu to taste
flawd flour
flin annoyed
flinedig tired
flodau flowers
flwch box
flwydd year
flwyddyn year
flychau boxes
flynedd years
flynyddoedd years
flynyddol annual
fo[1] he, him, it
    fo'i he him
fo[2] (he/she/it) should, may be
foch[1] cheek
foch[2] pigs
focs box
fod[1] to be
fod[2] that
fodd[1] satisfaction
fodd[2] means, way
foddhad satisfaction
foddhaol satisfactory
foddi to drown

foddion medicine
fodel model
fodelau models
fodern modem
foderneiddio to modernise
fodiwlau modules
fodlon satisfied
fodloni to satisfy
fodolaeth existence
fodolai (he/she/it would/used to) exist
fodoli to exist
fodrwy ring
fodryb aunt
foel bald, bare
foesol moral
fol belly, stomach
foltedd voltage
foment moment
fôn base, root
fonitro monitor
fôr sea
ford table
fordaith voyage
fore[1] a.m., morning
fore[2] early
forgais mortgage
forwyn maid, virgin
fory tomorrow
fotwm button
fraich arm
fraint honour
fras coarse, fat, general
fraster fat
frawd brother
frawddeg sentence
frawddegau sentences

frecwast breakfast
fregus shaky
freichiau arms
frenhines queen
frenhiniaeth kingdom
frenhinol royal
frenin king
frest chest
freuddwyd dream
freuddwydion dreams
fri honour, respect
fridio to breed
frig tip, top
frigâd brigade
frith[1] abundant
frith[2] dubious, shady
frith[3] mottled, speckled
frith[4] faint
fro area, vale
frodorol native
frodyr brothers
fron breast
frown brown
frwd keen
frwdfrydedd enthusiasm
frwdfrydig enthusiastic
frwydr battle
frwydro to battle
fry above, aloft
fryd mind, sights
fryn hill
fryngaer hill-fort
fryniau hills
frys haste
fu was, were
fuan quick, soon
fuasai (he/she/it) would have

fuaswn (I) would have
fuches milking herd
fud mute
fudd benefit
fudd-daliadau benefits
fuddiannau assets
fuddiant benefit
fuddiol useful
fuddsoddi to invest
fuddsoddiad investment
fuddsoddiadau investments
fuddugol victorious
fuddugoliaeth victories
fudiad movement
fudiadau movements
funud minute
funudau minutes
fuodd was, were
fur wall
furiau walls
fusnes business
fusnesau businesses
fuwch cow
fwg smoke
fwlch gap
fwlio to bully
fwrdd table
fwrdeistref borough
fwriad intention
fwriadol intentional
fwriadu to intend
fwriadwyd (was) intended
fwriedir (is) intended
fwrlwm bubbling
fwrw[1] to rain, to snow
fwrw[2] to hit
fws bus

fwthyn cottage
fwy bigger, more
fwyaf biggest, greatest
fwyafrif majority
fwyd food
fwydlen menu
fwydo to feed
fwydydd food, foodstuffs
fwyfwy ever more
fwyn gentle, mineral
fwynau minerals
fwynhad enjoyment
fwynhau to enjoy
fwyta to eat
fy my, me
fychan small
fyd world
fydd will, will be
fydda (I) shall, will
fyddaf (I) shall, will
fyddai (he/she/it) used to, would
fyddan (they) will
fyddant (they) will
fyddar deaf
fyddech (you) used to, would
fyddem (we) used to, would
fydden (they) used to, would
fyddent (they) used to, would
fyddi (you) will
fyddin army
fyddo (he/she/it) should
fyddwch (you) will
fyddwn (we) shall, will
fyd-eang world-wide
fyfyrio to meditate
fyfyriwr student
fyfyrwraig student (female)

fyfyrwyr students
fygwth to threaten
fygythiad threat
fygythiol threatening
fylchau gaps
fymryn little, touch of
fynd to go, to depart, to travel, to take, to become
fyned to go, to depart, to travel, to take, to become
fynedfa entrance
fynediad entrance
fynegai index
fynegi to express
fynegiant expression
fynegir (is/will be) expressed
fynegwyd (was) expressed
fynnai (he/she/it would/used to) insist
fynnir (is/will be) insisted
fynnu to insist
fynwent cemetery

fynwes breast
fyny up, upwards
fynych frequent
fynychaf most frequently
fynychu to frequent
fynydd mountain
fynyddoedd mountains
fyr short
fyrddau boards, tables
fyrder haste
fys finger
fysedd fingers
fysiau buses
fyth ever, never
fyw[1] to live
fyw[2] alive, live, lively, living
fywiog lively, vivacious
fywoliaeth livelihood
fywyd life, lifetime, verve
fywydau lives
ffrwyn bridle

G : g

---

a word starting with **g** printed in *italics* means that the root form
of that word begins with **c**, e.g. *gadair* root **cadair**

---

gad (you) leave!
gadael to leave, to allow,
    to bequeath
gadair chair
gadarn firm
gadarnhaol affirmative
gadarnhau to confirm
gadawodd (he/she/it) left
gadawyd (was) left
gadeiriau chairs
gadeirio to chair
gadeiriol chaired
gadeirlan cathedral
gadeirydd chairman
gadeiryddiaeth chairmanship
gadewch (you) leave, allow
gadw to keep
gadwraeth conservation
gadwyd¹ (was) left
gadwyd² (was) kept
gadwyn chain
gae¹ field
gae² (he/she/it) shuts
gaeaf winter
gaeau fields
gael to have
gaer fort
gaeth addicted, captive
gaf (I/I will) be allowed, have
gafael¹ to grasp, to grip
gafael² grasp, grip, hold

gaffael to acquire
gaffaeliad asset, acquisition
gafodd (he/she/it) had, was allowed
gafr goat
gafwyd (was) had
gâi (he/she/it would/used to) be
    allowed, have
gaiff (he/she/it will) be allowed,
    have
gain fine
gair promise, saying, word
gais¹ (he/she/it) seeks
gais² try
gal penis
galar grief, mourning
galaru to grieve, to mourn
galch chalk, lime
galed hard
galendr calendar
gall¹ (he/she/it) can, is able
gall² sensible, smart
gallaf¹ (I) am able, can
gallaf² wisest
gallai (he/she/it would/used to)
    be able
gallan (they) are able, can
gallant (they) are able, can
gallasai (he/she/it would have)
    been able
gallech (you would/used to)
    be able

gallem (we would/used to) be able

gallen (they would/used to) be able

gallent (they would/used to) be able

gallt hill, slope, wood

gallu[1] to be able

gallu[2] ability, force, power

galluoedd abilities

galluog able, clever, gifted

galluogi to enable

gallwch (you) are able, can

gallwn[1] (we) are able, can

gallwn[2] (I would/used to) be able

galon heart

galonogol encouraging

galw[1] call, demand

galw[2] to call, to telephone, to wake

galwad call, visit

galwadau calls

galwch (you) call

galwedigaeth calling, vocation

galwedigaethol occupational, vocational

galwodd (he/she/it) called

galwr caller

galwyd (was) called

gam[1] footprint, step

gam[2] wrong

gam[3] crooked, incorrect

gam[4] cam

gamarweiniol misleading

gamau[1] steps

gamau[2] wrongs

gamddefnyddio to misuse

gam-drin to abuse

gamdriniaeth abuse

gamfa stile

gamgymeriad mistake

gamgymeriadau mistakes

gamlas canal

gamp feat

gampws campus

gamu[1] to pace, to step

gamu[2] to bend, to distort

gamweinyddu to maladminister

gamymddwyn to misbehave

gan[1] by, from, have, of, with

gan[2] because, since

gan[3] hundred

gân song

ganddi by her, from her/it, of her/it, she has, with her

ganddo by him, from him/it, of him/it, he has, with him

ganddyn by them, from them, of them, they have, with them

ganddynt by them, from them, of them, they have, with them

ganed (was) born

ganeuon songs

ganfod to discover

ganfuwyd (was) discovered, perceived

ganfyddiadau discoveries

gang gang

gangen branch

ganghellor chancellor

ganghennau branches

ganiatâd permission

ganiataol granted

ganiatáu to allow, to permit

ganiateir (is/will be) allowed, permitted
ganllaw guideline
ganllawiau guidelines
ganlyn to follow
ganlyniad result
ganlyniadau results
ganlynol following
ganmol to praise
ganmoliaeth praise
gannoedd hundreds
gannwyll candle
ganodd (he/she/it) sang
ganol middle
ganolbwynt centre, focus
ganolbwyntio to focus
ganolfan centre
ganolfannau centres
ganolig mediocre, middling, moderate
ganoloesol medieval
ganolog central
ganran per cent
ganrif century
ganrifoedd centuries
ganser cancer
ganslo to cancel
gant hundred
gânt (they/they will) have
ganu to sing
ganwyd[1] (was) born
ganwyd[2] (was) sung
gap cap
gapel chapel
gapten captain
gar car
gâr kinsman

garchar prison
garcharor prisoner
garcharorion prisoners
gardd garden
garddio to garden
gardiau cards
garedig kind
garedigrwydd kindness
garej garage
garfan faction, squad
gariad love
gario to carry
garlamu to gallop
garreg stone
gartre home
gartref home
gartrefi homes
gartrefol homely
garu to love
garw harsh, rough, stormy, unrefined
gas nasty
gasgliad[1] collection, gathering
gasgliad[2] conclusion
gasgliadau[1] collections, gatherings
gasgliadau[2] conclusions
gasglu[1] to collect, to congregate
gasglu[2] to conclude
gasglu[3] to fester
gasglwyd[1] (was) collected, gathered
gasglwyd[2] (was) concluded
gastell castle
gât gate
gategori category
gategorïau categories
gath cat

gatiau gates
gau[1] false, hollow
gau[2] to close
gawl[1] soup
gawl[2] mess,
gawn (we will) be allowed, have
gawod shower
gaws cheese
gawsai (he/she/it) had, was allowed
gawsant (they) had, were allowed
gawsoch (you) had, were allowed
gawsom (we) had, were allowed
gawson (they) had, were allowed
gedwir (is/will be) kept
gefais (I) had, was allowed
geffyl horse
geffylau horses
gefn back
gefndir background
gefndiroedd backgrounds, settings
gefnogaeth support
gefnogi to support
gefnogir (is/will be) supported
gefnogol supportive
gefnogwyr supporters
geg mouth
gegin kitchen
gei (you will) be allowed, have
geid (would be/used to be) had, allowed
geidwad keeper, Saviour
geidwadol conservative
geifr goats
geiniog penny
geir[1] cars
geir[2] (is to be) allowed, had

geirfa glossary, vocabulary
geiriad wording
geiriadur dictionary
geiriaduron dictionaries
geiriau words
geiriol oral, verbal
geisiadau requests
geisio to seek
geisiodd (he/she/it) attempted
gelf art
gelfydd artistic
gelfyddyd art
gell cell
gelli[1] (you) are able, can
gelli[2] copse, grove
gellid (would/used to) be able
gellir (is/will be) able
gelloedd cells
gellwch (you) are able, can
gelwid (would be/used to be) called
gelwir (is/will be) called
gelyn[1] enemy, foe
gelyn[2] holly
gelynion enemies, foes
gem gem, jewel
gêm game, match
**gemau*[1]* gems
**gemau*[2]* games
**gen*[1]* by, from, have, of, with
**gen*[2]* dandruff, lichen
gên chin
genau entrance (of valley), mouth
genedigaeth birth
genedigaethau births
genedigol native
genedl gender, nation

genedlaethau generations
genedlaethol national
generig generic
geneteg genetics
geneth girl, lass
genethod girls
genetig genetic
genhadaeth mission
genhedlaeth generation
genhedloedd nations
geni to give birth to
gennych by you, from you, of you, with you, you have
gennyf by me, from me, of me, with me, I have
gennym by us, from us, of us, with us, we have
gennyt by you, from you, of you, with you, you have
ger by, close to, near
gerbron before, in the presence of
gerbyd carriage, vehicle
gerbydau carriages, vehicles
gerdd music, poem
gerdded to walk
gerddi[1] gardens
gerddi[2] poems
gerddorfa orchestra
gerddoriaeth music
gerddorol musical
gerddwyr walkers
gerdyn card
gerllaw beside, close to, near
gerrig stones
ges (I) had, was allowed
gesglir (is/will be) collected
gestyll castles

gewch (you will) be allowed, have
gi dog
gic kick
gig[1] gig
gig[2] meat
gilydd other, selves, together
ginio dinner
gipio to snatch
gist chest
gitâr guitar
gladdfa cemetery
gladdu to bury
glaf ill, patient
glan bank, side
glân[1] clean, fair, holy
glân[2] utter, complete
glanhau to clean
glanio to land
glannau banks
glanweithdra cleanliness
glas blue, green, grey, raw, young
glasurol classical
glaswellt grass, pasture
glaswelltir grassland
glaw rain, shower
glawiad rainfall
glawr cover, lid, surface
glefyd disease
glefydau diseases
gleientiaid clients
gleifion patients
gleision blue, blues
glendid beauty, cleanliness
glicio to click
glin knee, lap
glinigol clinical
glir clear

gliriach clearer
glirio to clear
glo[1] coal
glo[2] lock, conclusion
gloch bell
glod praise
gloddiau hedges
gloddio to dig
glofaol mining
gloi to lock
glos enclosure, farmyard
glòs close, near
glöwr coal-miner, collier
glowyr colliers
gloyw bright, sparkling
glud glue
gludiant transport
gludir (is/will be) carried, transported
gludo[1] to glue
gludo[2] to carry
glust ear
glustiau ears
glustnodi to earmark
glwb club
glwcos glucose
glybiau clubs
glymu to tie
glyn glen, vale, valley
glynu to stick
glyw[1] earshot, hearing
glyw[2] (he/she/it) hears
glywais (I) heard
glywed to hear
glywodd (he/she/it) heard
gnau nuts
gnawd flesh

gnwd crop
gnydau crops
go[1] partly, quite, rather
go[2] god!
go' memory
gobaith hope
gobeithio to hope
gobeithiol hopeful, optimistic
gobeithion hopes
gobeithir (is) hoped
gobeithiwn (we) hope
goblygiad consequence, implication
goblygiadau implications
goch red
goddef to allow, to put up with, to tolerate
goddefol passive
godi to raise, to lift, to build
godiad erection, increase
godidog excellent, magnificent, outstanding
godir (is/will be) raised
gododd (he/she/it) raised
godro to milk, to wheedle
godwyd (was) raised
goed trees, wood
goeden tree
goedwig forest
goedwigaeth forestry
goedwigoedd forests
goes handle, leg
goesau legs
goetir woodland
goetiroedd woodlands
gof[1] blacksmith, smith
gof[2] memory

gofal care, trouble
gofalu to look after, to make sure, to take care
gofalus careful, painstaking
gofalwch (you) make sure, take care
gofalwr caretaker, janitor
gofalwyr carers, caretakers
gofalydd carer
gofeb memorial
gofelir (is/will be) made sure, taken care
goffa memorial
goffi coffee
gofiadwy memorable
gofid distress, trouble, worry
gofidio to be anxious, to worry
gofio to remember
gofnod record
gofnodi to minute, to record
gofnodion minutes, records
gofnodir (is/will be) recorded
gofnodwyd (was) recorded
gofod space
gofodwr astronaut, cosmonaut, spaceman
gofodwyr astronauts
gofrestr register
gofrestredig registered
gofrestrfa registry
gofrestru to register
gofrestrwyd (was) registered
gofrestrydd registrar
gofyn[1] call, demand, request
gofyn[2] to ask, to invite, to require
gofyniad requirement
gofynion requirements

gofynnais (I) asked
gofynnir (is/will be) asked
gofynnodd (he/she/it) asked
gofynnol interrogative, necessary
gofynnwch (you) ask
gofynnwyd (was) asked
gog cuckoo
Gog North Walian
goginio to cook
gogledd north
gogledd-ddwyrain north-east
gogleddol northerly, northern
gogoniant glory, splendour
gogwydd bias, slant, tendency
gogyfer[1] facing, opposite
gogyfer[2] for, for the purpose of
gohebiaeth correspondence
gohebu to correspond, to report
gohebydd correspondent, journalist, reporter
gohirio to adjourn, to postpone
gohiriwyd (was) postponed
gol. ed., editor
gôl[1] goal
gôl[2] lap
golau[1] light
golau[2] bright, fair, light
golchi to wash
goleg college
golegau colleges
goleuadau lights
goleuni brightness, light
goleuo to enlighten, to light
golff golf
goll lost
golled loss, insanity
golledion losses

golli to lose
gollir (is/will be) lost
gollodd (he/she/it) lost
gollwng to drop, to leak, to release
gollwyd (was) lost
gollyngiad dispensation
gollyngiadau dispensations
golofn column
golosg charcoal, coke
golwg[1] sight, view, appearance, look
golwg[2] admiration, respect
golyga[1] (he/she/it will) mean
golyga[2] (he/she/it will) edit
golygai[1] (he/she/it would/ used to) mean
golygai[2] (he/she/it would/ used to) edit
golygfa scene, sight, view
golygfeydd views
golygir[1] (is/will be) meant
golygir[2] (is/will be) edited
golygu[1] to mean, to intend
golygu[2] to edit
golygwyd[1] (was) meant
golygwyd[2] (was) edited
golygydd editor
golygyddion editors
golygyddol editorial
gomisiwn commission
gomisiynu to commission
gomisiynwyd (was) commissioned
gonest frank, honest, true
gonestrwydd honesty
gontract contract
gontractau contracts

gontractwyr contractors
gopi copy
gopïau copies
gopïo to copy
gor[1] dwarf, midget, pygmy
gor[2] spider
gorau best
gorbwyso to be overweight, to outweigh
gorchfygu to conquer, to overcome
gorchmynion commands
gorchudd cover, lid, veil
gorchuddio to cover, to envelop
gorchwyl job, task
gorchwylion tasks
gorchymyn[1] command, decree, order
gorchymyn[2] to command
gore best
goresgyn to conquer, to invade, to vanquish
goreuon best
gorff body
gorffen to conclude, to end, to finish
gorffenedig completed, finished, perfected
gorffennaf (I/I will) finish
Gorffennaf July
gorffennol past, past tense
gorfforaeth corporation
gorfforaethol corporate
gorfforol physical
gorffwylledd dementia, insanity
gorffwys to repose, to rest
gorffwysfa caesura, resting place

gorfod¹ compulsion, constraint
gorfod² to be compelled to, to have to
gorfodaeth coercion, duress
gorfodi to compel, to force, to make
gorfodol compulsory, obligatory
gorfoledd jubilation, rejoicing
gorgyffwrdd to overlap
gorlawn overflowing
gorlifdir floodplain
gorlifo to flood, to inundate, to overflow
gorllewin west
gorllewinol westerly, western
gormes oppression, repression, tyranny
gormod¹ excess, much, too many
gormod² excessive, too much
gormodedd excess, glut
gormodol excessive, fulsome
gorn¹ horn, trumpet
gorn² horn, antler, callous
gorn³ maize
gorn⁴ absolute, complete
gornel corner
gornest bout, contest
goroesi to outlast, to outlive, to survive
goron crown, garland
goror border, frontier
gororau frontiers, Marches
gors bog, marsh
gorsaf depot, station
gorsafoedd stations
gorsedd throne

goruchwyliaeth stewardship, supervision
goruchwylio to oversee, to supervise
goruchwyliwr overseer, supervisor
gorwedd to lie, to rest
gorwel horizon
gorwelion horizons
gosb penalty, punishment
gosbi to punish
gosod¹ to set, to arrange, to let, to put
gosod² false, set
gosodiad setting, statement
gosodiadau settings, statements
gosodir (is/will be) set
gosododd (he/she/it) set
gosodwch (you) set
gosodwyd (was) set
gost cost
gostio to cost
gostus expensive
gostwng to bow, to lower, to reduce
gostyngiad fall, slump, subjugation
gostyngiadau reductions
gostyngol reduced
got coat, coating
gôt coat, coating
grac angry, annoyed
gradd degree, grade, order
graddau degrees, grades
graddedig graded, graduated
graddedigion graduates
graddfa scale
graddfeydd grades, scales

graddio to grade, to graduate
graddol gradual
graean gravel, shingle
graff[1] graph
graff[2] sharp, shrewd
graffeg graphics
graffiau graphs
graffig graphic
graffiti graffiti
graffito graffiti, graffito
gragen shell
graidd centre, crux, essence
graig rock
gram gram, gramme
gramadeg grammar
gramadegol grammatical
grand grand
grant grant
grantiau grants
gras[1] grace
gras[2] dry, harsh
grawn grain
greadigaeth creation
greadigol creative
greadur creature
greaduriaid creatures
gred belief
gredu to believe
gredyd credit
gredydau credits
gref strong
grefft craft
grefydd religion
grefyddol religious
greiddiol core, central, essential
greigiau rocks
greodd (he/she/it) created

grêt great
greu to create
greulon cruel
greulondeb cruelty
grëwyd (was) created
grib comb, ridge
grid grid
gridiau grids
grisiau staircase, stairs, steps
griw crew, gang
gro gravel, shingle, earth
Groeg Greek
groen skin
groes against, cross
groesawu to welcome
groesfan crossing
groesi to cross
groeso welcome
gron round
gronfa fund
gronfeydd funds
gronyn grain, granule, particle
gronynnau grains, particles
groth womb
grug[1] heather
grug[2] hillock
grwn round
grŵp group
grwpiau groups
grwpio to group
grwydro to wander
grybwyll to mention
grybwyllir (is/will be) mentioned
grybwyllwyd (was) mentioned
gryf strong
gryfach stronger
gryfder strength

gryfderau strengths
gryfhau to strengthen
grym force, strength, vigour
grymoedd forces
grymus mighty, powerful, strong
gryn quite, fair, pretty, tolerable
grynhoi[1] to assemble, to accumulate
grynhoi[2] to summarise
grynhoi[3] to fester
gryno compact, concise
grynodeb summary
grys shirt
gu beloved
gudd hidden
guddio to hide
gul narrow
guro to beat
gw. see
gwadd[1] mole
gwadd[2] guest
gwadiad denial
gwadu to deny, to disclaim, to disown
gwaddod sediment
gwaddodion lees
gwaddoliad endowment
gwae woe
gwaed blood, gore
gwaeddodd (he/she/it) shouted
gwaedlyd bloody
gwaedu to bleed, to let blood
gwael[1] poor
gwael[2] ill, poorly
gwaelod bottom, depths
gwaelodlin base line
gwaelodol basal

gwaered descent, downward slope
gwaeth worse
gwaetha worst
gwaethaf worst
gwaethygu to decay, to deteriorate
gwag empty, vacant
gwahân apart
gwahaniaeth difference, disagreement, distinction
gwahaniaethau differences
gwahaniaethol differentiating, distinguishing
gwahaniaethu to differ, to discriminate, to distinguish
gwahanol different, various
gwahanu to part, to separate, to split up
gwahardd to forbid, to prohibit
gwaharddiad ban, prohibition
gwaharddiadau bans, prohibitions
gwahodd to invite
gwahoddiad invitation
gwahoddir (is/will be) invited
gwahoddwyd (was) invited
gwair hay
gwaith[1] occasion, time
gwaith[2] task, work
gwalch[1] knave, rascal
gwalch[2] falcon, hawk
gwall error, mistake, oversight
gwallau errors
gwallt hair
gwan weak
gwanas buttress

gwanhau to languish, to weaken
gwanwyn spring
gwar scruff, nape
gwarant guarantee, warrant
gwarantau guarantees, warrants
gwarantu to guarantee,
    to underwrite
gwarchod to baby-sit, to guard,
    to look after
gwarchodaeth conservation,
    custodianship, protection
gwarchodfa reservation,
    reserve, sanctuary
gwared[1] to rid, to save
gwared[2] riddance
gwarediad deliverance, riddance
gwaredu to get rid of
gwareiddiad civilization
gwarged remainder, surplus
gwariant expenditure
gwario to spend
gwariwyd (was) spent
gwarth disgrace, scandal, shame
gwartheg cattle, kine
gwas farm-hand, lad, manservant
gwasanaeth service
gwasanaethau services
gwasanaethir (is/will be) served
gwasanaethu to officiate,
    to serve
gwasg[1] press
gwasg[2] waist
gwasgar dispersed
gwasgaredig dispersed, scattered
gwasgaru to disperse, to scatter
gwasgedd pressure
gwasgnod imprint

gwasgnodau imprints
gwasgu to press, to squeeze,
    to wring
gwastad[1] always, constant, flat,
    level
gwastad[2] flat, level, plain
gwastadedd level
gwastraff wastage, waste
gwastraffu to fritter, to waste
gwau[1] knitting
gwau[2] to knit, to spin, to weave
gwawd mockery, scorn
gwawr dawn, daybreak, sunrise,
    tone
gwawrio to dawn
gwbl complete
gwblhau to complete
gwblhawyd (was) completed
gwch boat
gwddf neck, throat
gwe cobweb, web
gwedd[1] appearance,
    countenance, sight
gwedd[2] harness, team, yoke
gweddi prayer
gweddïau prayers
gweddill remainder, surplus,
    (the) rest
gweddillion remnants
gweddïo to pray
gweddol fair, middling,
    reasonable
gweddu to fit, to suit
gweddw[1] widow
gweddw[2] widowed
gwefan website
gwefannau websites

gwefeistr webmaster
gwefr charge, shock, thrill
gwefus lip
gwefusau lips
gwe gamera web-cam
gweiddi to shout, to yell
gweill knitting-needles
gweini to attend, to be in
  service, to serve, to wait upon
gweinidog minister, pastor
gweinidogaeth ministry
gweinidogion ministers
gweinydd attendant, waiter
gweinyddiaeth administration,
  ministry
gweinyddir (is/will be)
  administered
gweinyddu to administer, to
  manage, to officiate
gweinyddwr administrator
gweinyddwyr administrators
gweinyddol administrative
gweision servants
gweithdai workshops
gweithdrefn procedure
gweithdrefnau procedures
gweithdy workshops
gweithfeydd works
gweithgar diligent, industrious
gweithgaredd activity
gweithgareddau activities
gweithgarwch activity, diligence,
  industry
gweithgor working party
gweithgorau working parties
gweithgynhyrchu to
  manufacture

gweithiau works
gweithio to work, to operate,
  to ferment
gweithiodd (he/she/it) worked
gweithiol operative, working
  class
gweithion (they) worked
gweithiwr labourer, worker
gweithle workplace
gweithlu manpower, workforce
gweithred action, deed,
  document
gweithrediad operation
gweithrediadau deeds,
  operations
gweithredir (is/will be) done
gweithredoedd deeds
gweithredol acting, executive
gweithredu to do, to implement
gweithredwr agent, operator
gweithredwyd (was) done
gweithredwyr operators
gweithredydd operator
gweithwyr workers
gwêl (he/she/it) sees, behold!
gweladwy visible
gwelaf (I/I will) see
gwelai (he/she/it would/used to)
  see
gwelais (I) saw
gweld to see, to seem, to
  understand, to visit
gweled to see
gweledigaeth brainwave, vision
gweledol visual
gwelem (we would/used to) see
gweler behold, see

gweli (you/you will) see
gwelid (would be/used to be)
    seen
gwelir (is/will be) seen
gwell[1] better, preferable
gwell[2] betters, superiors
gwella to get better, to improve,
    to make better
gwelliannau improvements
gwelliant amendment,
    improvement
gwellt straw
gwelodd (he/she/it) saw
gwelsant (they) saw
gwelsoch (you) saw
gwelsom (we) saw
gwelwch (you/you will) see
gwelwn (we/we will) see
gwelwyd (was) seen
gwely bed
gwelyau beds
gwen white
gwên smile
gwendid fault, infirmity, weakness
gwendidau weaknesses
Gwener[1] Friday
Gwener[2] Venus
gwenith wheat
gwennol shuttle, shuttlecock,
    swallow
gwenu to grin, to shine, to smile
gwenwyn poison, spite, spleen,
    venom
gwenwynig poisonous,
    venomous
gwenyn bees
gwenynen bee

gwêr grease, tallow, wax
gwerdd green
gwerin[1] chessmen, pieces
gwerin[2] folk
gweriniaeth republic
gwerinol common, plebeian
gwern[1] alders
gwern[2] quagmire, swamp
gwers lesson
gwersi lessons
gwersyll camp
gwersylloedd camps
gwerth[1] value
gwerth[2] worth
gwerthfawr precious, valuable
gwerthfawrogi to appreciate,
    to value
gwerthfawrogiad appreciation,
    gratitude
gwerthiannau sales
gwerthiant sale
gwerthir (is/will be) sold
gwerthodd (he/she/it) sold
gwerthoedd values
gwerthu to sell, to vend
gwerthusiad appraisal
gwerthusiadau appraisals
gwerthuso to appraise
gwerthwr salesman, seller
gwerthwyd (was) sold
gwerthwyr sellers
gwestai guest
gwesteion guests
gwestiwn question
gwestiynau questions
gwesty boarding-house, guest
    house, hotel

gweundir moorland
gwialen cane, rod, sapling
gwibio to dart, to flit, to rush
gwichian to squeal
gwifrau wires
gwifren wire
gwin wine
gwir[1] truth
gwir[2] genuine, real, true
gwir[3] really, truly
gwireddu to come true, to make true
gwirfoddol voluntary, willing
gwirfoddoli to volunteer
gwirfoddolwr volunteer
gwirfoddolwyr volunteers
gwiriadau corrections
gwirio to check, to swear, to verify
gwirion daft, guileless, silly, simple, stupid
gwirionedd truth
gwirioneddol genuine, real, true
gwiriwch (you) check
gwisg clothing, costume, dress
gwisgo to dress, to wear
gwisgoedd costumes
gwiw excellent, fine, worthy
gwiwer squirrel
gwiwerod squirrels
gwlad country, countryside, nation
gwladfa colony, settlement
gwladol state
gwladwriaeth state
gwladwriaethau states
gwladychu to colonise, to inhabit

gwlân wool, woollen
gwledd banquet, feast, treat
gwledig country, rural
gwledydd countries
gwleidydd politician
gwleidyddiaeth politics
gwleidyddion politicians
gwleidyddol political
gwlith dew
gwlyb wet
gwlyptiroedd wetlands
gwm[1] glue, gum
gwm[2] valley
gwmni company
gwmnïau companies
gwmpas[1] around
gwmpas[2] compass
gwmpasu to encompass
gwmwl cloud
gwn[1] gun
gwn[2] (I) know
gŵn[1] gown
gŵn[2] dogs
gwna[1] (he/she/it) does, makes
gwna[2] (you) do!, make!
gwnaed (was) done, made
gwnaeth (he/she/it) did, made
gwnaethant (they) did, made
gwnaethoch (you) did, made
gwnaethom (we) did, made
gwnaethon (they) did, made
gwnaethpwyd (was) done, made
gwnaf (I/I will) do, make
gwnâi (he/she/it) did, made
gwnaiff (he/she/it would/ used to) do, make

gwnânt (they/they will) do, make
gwnawn (we/we will) do, make
gwnei (you/you will) do, make
gwneid (would be/used to be) done, made
gwneir (is/will be) done, made
gwnelo (he/she/it were to/might) do, make
gwnes (I) did, made
gwneud[1] to do, to force, to make
gwneud[2] false
gwneuthur to make
gwneuthurwr maker, manufacturer
gwneuthurwyr makers
gwnewch (you) do, make
gwnstabl constable
gwobr award, prize, reward
gwobrau prizes
gwobrwyo to award a prize, to reward
gwpan cup
gwr edge
gŵr husband, man
gwrach hag, witch
gwrachen loach, wrasse
gwrachod witches
gwragedd wives, women
gwraidd origin, root, source
gwraig wife, woman
gwrandawiad audition, hearing
gwrandawiadau hearings
gwrandawr listener
gwrandawyr listeners
gwrandewch (you) listen
gwrando to listen
gwrdd[1] meeting, service

gwrdd[2] to meet, to touch
gwreichion sparks
gwreiddiau roots
gwreiddiol fresh, original
gwreiddyn origin, reason, root
gwres fever, heat, intensity, temperature
gwresogi to heat
gwrs[1] chase, course
gwrs[2] coarse
gwrtais polite
gwrtaith fertiliser, manure
gwrthdaro to clash, to collide
gwrthgyferbyniad contrast, opposition
gwrthiant resistance
gwrthod to refuse, to reject
gwrthododd (he/she/it) refused
gwrthodwyd (was) refused
gwrthrych object
gwrthrychau objects
gwrthrychol objective
gwrthryfel mutiny, rebellion, revolt
gwrthsefyll to thwart, to withstand
gwrthwyneb contrary, opposite, reverse
gwrthwynebiad objection, opposition, resistance
gwrthwynebiadau objections
gwrthwynebu to be opposed to, to object, to oppose, to resist
gwrthwynebwyr opponents
gwrthwynebydd adversary, objector, opponent

gwrw beer
gwrych hedge, bristles
gwrychoedd hedges
gwryw male
gwrywaidd masculine
gwsg sleep
gwsmer customer
gwsmeriaid customers
gwthio to push, to shove, to thrust
gwtogi to reduce
Gwy Wye (river)
gwybod to know
gwybodaeth information, knowledge
gwybodus enlightened, learned, well-informed
gwybyddus known
gwych excellent, gorgeous, magnificent
gŵydd goose
gwyddai (he/she/it would/ used to) know
Gwyddel Irishman
Gwyddeleg Irish (language)
Gwyddelig Irish
Gwyddelod Irish (people)
gwyddoch (you) know
gwyddom (we) know
gwyddoniaeth science
gwyddonol scientific
gwyddonwyr scientists
gwyddonydd scientist
gwyddor first principles, rudiments, science
gwyddorau sciences
gwyddost (you) know

gwyddwn (I would/used to) know
Gwyddyl Irishmen
gwyddys (it is) known
gwydr glass, tumbler
gwydrau glasses, tumblers
gŵyl[1] festival, modest
gŵyl[2] modest
gwyliadwriaeth alertness, guard, vigilance, wariness, watch
gwyliadwrus alert, wary, watchful
gwyliau holidays, leave, vacation
gwylio to beware, to keep watch, to look out, to observe, to take care of, to tend, to watch
gwyliwch (you) watch, beware!
gwyliwr guard, sentry, spectator, viewer, watcher
gwyll dusk, gloom, twilight
gwyllt wild, raging, rash
gwylltion wild
gwylwyr spectators, viewers
gwympo to fall
gwyn white, blessed, silver
gŵyn complaint
gwynfa paradise
gwynion[1] white
gwynion[2] complaints
gwyno to complain
gwynt breath, flatulence, smell, wind
gwyntoedd winds
gŵyr men
gŵyr[1] (he/she/it) knows
gŵyr[2] crooked, slanting
gŵyr[3] wax

gwyrdd green, unripe
gwyrddion green, greens
gwyro[1] to bend, to distort,
  to incline, to veer
gwyro[2] to wax
gwyrth miracle
gwythïen seam, vein
gwythiennau veins
gychod boats
gychwyn to start
gychwynnodd (he/she/it) started
gychwynnol first, starting
gyd all
gyda along, with
  gyda'ch with your
  gyda'i with his/her/its
  gyda'u with their
gydag along, with
gydau bags
gydbwysedd balance
gyd-destun context
gyd-destunau contexts
gyd-fynd to agree
gydlynol cohesive
gydlynu to coordinate
gydlynus coordinative
gydnabod to acknowledge
gydnabyddiaeth
  acknowledgement
gydnabyddir (is/will be)
  acknowledged
gydnaws compatible
gydol whole
gydradd equal
gydraddoldeb equality
gydran component
gydrannau components

gydsyniad agreement
gydweithio to cooperate
gydweithrediad cooperation
gydweithredol cooperative
gydweithredu to cooperate
gydweithwyr colleagues
gydwybod conscience
gydymdeimlad sympathy
gydymffurfio to conform
gyfaddas suitable
gyfaddef to admit
gyfadran faculty
gyfagos adjoining
gyfaill friend
gyfaint volume
gyfalaf capital
gyfan whole
gyfanrwydd totality
gyfansoddi to compose
gyfansoddiad composition
gyfanswm sum, total
gyfarch to greet
gyfarfod meeting
gyfarfodydd meetings
gyfarpar apparatus
gyfartal equal
gyfartaledd average
gyfarwydd familiar
gyfarwyddeb directive
gyfarwyddiadau directions
gyfarwyddiaeth directorship
gyfarwyddo to direct
gyfarwyddwr director
gyfarwyddwraig director (female)
gyfarwyddwyr directors
gyfarwyddyd direction
gyfateb to correspond

gyfatebol corresponding
gyfathrebu to communicate
gyfeillgar amicable
gyfeillion friends
gyfeiriad[1] address, reference
gyfeiriad[2] direction
gyfeiriadau[1] addresses, references
gyfeiriadau[2] directions
gyfeirio[1] to direct
gyfeirio[2] to reference
gyfer[1] acre
gyfer[2] behalf
gyfer[3] headlong
gyferbyn opposite
gyffelyb like
gyffordd junction
gyfforddus comfortable
gyffredin common
gyffredinol general
gyffro excitement
gyffrous exciting
gyffuriau drugs
gyffwrdd to touch
gyfiawn just
gyfiawnder justice
gyfiawnhad justification
gyfiawnhau to justify
gyfieithiad translation
gyfieithu to translate
gyflawn[1] complete
gyflawn[2] intransitive
gyflawni to accomplish
gyflawniad accomplishment
gyflawnir (is/will be) accomplished
gyflawnodd (he/she/it) accomplished
gyflawnwyd (was) accomplished

gyfle chance
gyflenwad supply
gyflenwi to supply
gyflenwyr suppliers
gyfleoedd opportunities
gyfleu to convey
gyfleus convenient
gyfleuster convenience
gyfleusterau conveniences
gyflog salary
gyflogaeth employment
gyflogau wages
gyflogedig employed
gyflogi to employ
gyflogir (is/will be) employed
gyflogwr employer
gyflogwyr employers
gyflwr condition
gyflwyniad presentation
gyflwyniadau presentations
gyflwynir (is/will be) presented
gyflwyno to present
gyflwynodd (he/she/it) presented
gyflwynwyd (was) presented
gyflym fast
gyflymach faster
gyflymder speed
gyfnewid to exchange
gyfnod period
gyfnodau periods
gyfochrog parallel
gyfoedion contemporaries
gyfoes contemporary
gyfoeth wealth
gyfoethog wealthy
gyfoethogi to enrich
gyfradd rate

gyfraddau rates
gyfraith law
gyfran share
gyfraniad contribution
gyfraniadau contributions
gyfrannodd (he/she/it) contributed
gyfrannol contributory, proportional
gyfrannu to contribute
gyfranogi to partake of
gyfranogiad participation
gyfranogwyr participator
gyfranwyr contributors
gyfredol current
gyfreithiol legal
gyfreithiwr lawyer
gyfreithlon legitimate
gyfreithwyr lawyers
gyfres series
gyfrif account
gyfrifiadur computer
gyfrifiadurol computer
gyfrifiaduron computers
gyfrifir (is/will be) calculated
gyfrifo to calculate
gyfrifol responsible
gyfrifoldeb responsibility
gyfrifoldebau responsibilities
gyfrifon accounts
gyfrinach secret
gyfrinachol secret
gyfrol volume
gyfrolau volumes
gyfrwng medium
gyfryngau media
gyfun comprehensive

gyfundrefn system
gyfundrefnol systemic
gyfuniad combination
gyfuno to combine
gyfunol combined
gyfweliad interview
gyfweliadau interviews
gyfwerth equal
gyfyd (he/she/it) lifts
gyfyng narrow
gyfyngedig restricted
gyfyngiad limit
gyfyngiadau limits
gyfyngu to limit
gyfystyr synonymous
gyhoeddi to publish
gyhoeddiad publication
gyhoeddiadau publications
gyhoeddir (is/will be) announced, published
gyhoeddodd (he/she/it) announced, published
gyhoeddus public
gyhoeddusrwydd publicity
gyhoeddwyd (was) announced, published
gyhuddo to accuse
gylch circle
gylchgrawn magazine
gylchgronau magazines
gylchoedd circles
gyllell knife
gyllid revenue
gyllideb budget
gyllidebau budgets
gyllidir (is/will be) financed
gyllido to finance

gymaint as much
gymal clause, joint
gymanwlad commonwealth
gymdeithas society
gymdeithasau societies
gymdeithasol social
gymdeithasu to socialise
gymdogaeth neighbourhood
gymdogion neighbours
gymer (he/she/it) takes
gymeradwy acceptable
gymeradwyaeth applause
gymeradwyir (is/will be) approved
gymeradwyo to approve
gymeradwywyd (was) approved
gymeriad character
gymeriadau characters
gymerir (is/will be) taken
gymerodd (he/she/it) took
gymerwyd (was) taken
gymesur symmetrical
gymhareb ratio
gymhariaeth comparison
gymharol comparative
gymharu to compare
gymhelliad incentive
gymhleth complex
gymhwyso to adapt
gymhwyster qualification
gymorth aid
Gymraeg Welsh
Gymraes Welshwoman
Gymreig Welsh
Gymro Welshman
Gymru Wales
Gymry Welsh people
gymryd to take

gymuned community
gymunedau communities
gymunedol community
gymwys suitable
gymwysterau qualifications
gymydog neighbour
gymysg mixed
gymysgedd mixture
gymysgu to mix
gynaliadwy sustainable
gyndyn reticent
gynefin habitat
gynefinoedd habitats
gynffon[1] appendage, tail
gynffon[2] tang, aftertaste
gyngerdd concert
gynghanedd harmony, Welsh poetic alliteration
gynghorau councils
gynghori to advise
gynghorwyr councillors
gynghorydd councillor
gynghrair league
gyngor council, counsel
gynhadledd conference
gynhaliaeth subsistence
gynhaliwyd (was) held
gynharach earlier
gynhelir (is/will be) held
gynhenid inherent
gynhesu to warm
gynhwysfawr comprehensive
gynhwysion contents
gynhwysir (is/will be) included
gynhwysol inclusive
gynhwyswyd (was) included
gynhyrchion products

gynhyrchir (is/will be) produced
gynhyrchu to produce
gynhyrchwyd (was) produced
gynhyrchwyr producers
gynifer as many
gynigion attempts, offers
gynigir (is/will be) offered, proposed
gynigiwyd (was) offered, proposed
gynilion savings
gynilo to save
gynllun plan
gynlluniau plans
gynllunio to plan
gynlluniwyd (was) planned
gynnal to hold
gynnar early
gynnau[1] guns
gynnau[2] earlier
gynnau[3] to light
gynnes warm
gynnig offer, proposal, try
gynnil sparing
gynnwys to include
gynnydd growth
gynnyrch produce
gynorthwyo to assist
gynradd primary
gynrychiolaeth representation
gynrychioli to represent
gynrychiolir (is/will be) represented
gynrychiolwyr representatives
gynrychiolydd representative
gynt previously, quicker
gyntaf first

gynted as soon
gynulleidfa audience, congregation
gynulleidfaoedd audiences
gynulliad assembly
gynwysedig included
gynyddol increasing
gynyddu to increase
gyrchfan destination
gyrchu to make for
gyrfa career, drive
gyrfaoedd careers
gyrfaol vocational
gyrff bodies
gyrhaeddiad reach
gyrhaeddodd (he/she/it) reached
gyrion outskirts
gyrraedd to reach
gyrru to dispatch, to drive, to send
gyrrwr driver, drover
gyrsiau courses
gyrwyr drivers
gysegredig sacred
gysgod shadow
gysgu to sleep
gyson constant
gystadlaethau competitions
gystadleuaeth competition
gystadleuol competitive
gystadleuwyr competitors
gystadlu to compete
gystal as good as
gysur comfort
gysurus comfortable
gyswllt contact
gysylltiad connection, link

gysylltiadau links
gysylltiedig linked
gysylltir (is/will be) contacted, connected
gysylltu to contact, to link
gysyniad concept
gysyniadau concepts
gytbwys balanced
gytsain consonant

gytundeb agreement, contract
gytundebau contracts
gytuno to agree
gytunwyd (was) agreed
gywilydd shame
gywir correct
gywirdeb accuracy
gywiro to correct

H : h

a word starting with **h** printed in *italics* means that the root form
of that word begins with the second letter of the word,
e.g. *hachos* root **achos**, *hoed* root **oed**

ha hectare
hachos case, cause
hachosi to cause
hachub to save
had seed, sperm
hadau seeds
haddasu to adapt
haddysg education
haddysgu to educate
hadeiladau buildings
hadeiladu to build
hadfer to recover, to restore
hadlewyrchu to reflect
hadnabod to know, to recognise
hadnewyddu to renew
hadnoddau resources
hadolygiad review
hadolygu to review
hadran department, section
hadrodd to recite, to report
hadroddiad report
haearn iron
haeddiannol deserved,
  deserving
haeddiant deserts, merit
haeddu to deserve, to merit
hael[1] generous, lavish,
  magnanimous
hael[2] eyebrow
haelioni generosity

haelodau members
haen bed, coating, layer, stratum
haenau layers
haenen layer
haf summer
hafal[1] comparable, equal
hafal[2] apple
hafaliad equation, formula
hafaliadau equations, formulae
hafan haven, home page
hafau summers
hafod summer dwelling/pasture
Hafren Severn (river)
hagor to open
hagwedd attitude
haid flock, group, horde, swarm
haidd barley
hail second
hailgylchu to recycle
haint disease, fit, pestilence
halen salt
hallt[1] salty, harsh, steep
hallt[2] hill, wood
halogi to corrupt, to defile,
  to desecrate
hamcanion intentions
hamdden leisure, pastime
hamddena to relax
hamddenol leisurely
hamddiffyn to defend

hamgylch around
hamgylchedd environment
hamgylchiadau circumstances
hamlygu to reveal
hamser time
hanafu to injure
hanelu to aim
hanes account, history, report,
   story, tale
hanesion stories
haneswyr historians
hanesydd historian
hanesyddol historic, historical
hanfod essence, quintessence
hanfodion essentials
hanfodol crucial, essential, vital
hanfon to send
hangen to need
hanghenion necessities
haniaethol abstract
hanifeiliaid animals
hanner half
hannibyniaeth independence
hannog to urge
hanwybyddu to ignore
hap chance, fortune, luck
hapus happy
hapusrwydd happiness
harbenigedd expertise
harbwr harbour
harchwiliad investigation
harchwilio to investigate
hardal area
hardaloedd areas
hardd beautiful, fair, handsome
harddangos to display
harddegau teens

harddwch beauty
harfer custom
harferion customs
harglwydd lord
hargraffu to print
hargymell to recommend
hargymhellion
   recommendations
harian money, silver
hariannu to finance
harolwg survey
harolygu to inspect, to review
harwain to lead
hasesu to assess
hastudiaethau studies
hastudio to study
hatal to prevent
hateb[1] to answer, to reply
hateb[2] answer, reply, solution
hategu to support
hatgoffa to remind
hatgynhyrchu to reproduce
hau to sow
haul sun
hawdd easy, ready
hawdurdod authority
hawdurdodi to authorise
hawl right
hawlfraint copyright
hawliad claim
hawliadau claims
hawliau rights
hawlio to claim, to demand
haws easier
heb not, without
hebddo without him
heblaw apart from, besides

121

Hebraeg Hebrew
hebrwng to escort
hectar hectare
hedd peace
heddiw today, nowadays
heddlu constabulary, police force
heddluoedd police forces
heddwch peace, tranquillity
heddychlon peaceful
hedfan to fly, to soar
hedodd (he/she/it) flew
heffaith effect
heffeithio to effect
heffeithiolrwydd efficiency
hefo together with, with
    hefo'i with his/her/its
hefyd also, too
heglwysi churches
hei hey!
heibio by, past
heiddo possessions, property
heini active, spry, vigorous
heintiad infection
heintiau infections
heintiedig infected
heintio to contaminate, to infect
heintus catching, contagious,
    infectious
heithrio to except
hel to collect, to gather, to send
hela to hunt, to spend
helaeth extensive, large, plentiful
helaethach more extensive
helaethaf most extensive
helfa catch, hunt
heli[1] briny, sea
heli[2] balm, ointment

helô hello
help aid, help
helpu to help
helyg willows
helynt bother, predicament,
    trouble
helyntion troubles
hen ancient, former, old, stale
henaid soul
henaint old age, senility
hendre winter dwelling or pasture
heneb monument
henebion ancient monuments
heneiddio to age, to become old
Henffordd Hereford
hennill to win
heno tonight
henoed old age, old people
henw name
henwau names
henwebu to nominate
henwi to name
heol road
heolydd roads
hepgor to avoid, to forego
her challenge, dare
herbyn against
herian to brave, to challenge,
    to defy
heriau challenges, dares
herio to challenge
heriol challenging
herwydd because
het hat
hethol to elect
heulog sunny
heulwen sunshine

hi she, it
hiaith language
hidlo to filter, to percolate, to strain
hiechyd health
hil descendants, offspring, race
hiliaeth racism
hiliol racial, racist
hin weather
hincwm income
hinsawdd climate
hintegreiddio to integrate
hir long, tedious
hirach longer
hiraeth homesickness, nostalgia
hirdymor long-term
hirion long
his lower
hithau herself
hiwmor humour
hochr side
hoed age
hoedran age
hoelen nail
hoelio to nail, to rivet
hoelion nails
hoes age, lifetime
hoff beloved, dear, favourite
hoffai (he/she/it would/ used to) like
hoffech (you would/used to) like
hoffem (we would/used to) like
hoffent (they would/used to) like
hoffi to like, to wish
hoffter fondness, liking
hoffwn[1] (I would/used to) like
hoffwn[2] (we/we will) like

hofrenydd helicopter
hogan girl
hogen girl
hogia' lads
hogiau lads
hogyn lad
hôl[1] behind
hôl[2] impression, track
holau behind
holi to ask, to inquire, to question
holiadur questionnaire
holiaduron questionnaires
holl all, whole
hollbwysig all-important
hollol entire, quite, whole
hollt cleavage, cleft, cranny, split
hollti to cleave, to split
holodd (he/she/it) asked
holwch (you) ask
holwyd (was) asked
hon this
honedig alleged
hongian to hang, to suspend
honiad allegation, assertion, claim
honiadau allegations
honni to allege, to claim, to maintain
honnir (is/will be) claimed
honno that one
hosgoi to avoid
hoyw gay, lively, vivacious
huawdl eloquent, loquacious
hud magic, enchantment
hudo to charm, to conjure, to enchant
hudol alluring, enchanting, magical
hudolus enchanting

hufen cream
hugain twenty
hun[1] self
hun[2] sleep, slumber
hunain selves
hunan self
hunanasesiad self-assessment
hunanasesu to assess oneself
hunan-barch self-respect
hunangofiant autobiography, memoirs
hunangyflogedig self-employed
hunaniaeth identity
hunanladdiad suicide
hunig lonely, only
hunllef nightmare
huno[1] to sleep, to slumber
huno[2] to amalgamate, to join, to unite
hurio to hire
hurt silly, stunned, stupid
hwb push, shove
hwch sow
hwn this
hwnna that
hwnnw that
hwnt away, yonder
hwrdd[1] ram
hwrdd[2] gust, squall
hwy[1] them, they
hwy[2] longer
hwy[3] egg
hwyaid ducks
hwyl[1] fun
hwyl[1] goodbye
hwyl[3] mood
hwyl[4] sail

hwyliau[1] sails
hwyliau[2] good mood
hwylio to get ready, to prepare, to sail, to wheel
hwyliog humorous
hwylus convenient, handy, healthy
hwyluso to expedite, to facilitate
hwylustod convenience
hwyneb face
hwynebau faces
hwynebu to face
hwynt them
hwyr[1] late, overdue
hwyr[2] evening
hwyrach[1] maybe, perhaps
hwyrach[2] later
hwythau themselves
hy bold, impudent, presumptuous
hyblyg flexible, pliable, supple
hyblygrwydd flexibility, suppleness
hybu to encourage, to improve, to promote, to recover
hychwanegu to add
hyd[1] duration, length
hyd[2] along, as far as, until, up to
hyd[3] as long as
hyddysg expert, learned
hyder confidence
hyderus confident, sanguine
hydref autumn
Hydref October
hydrogen hydrogen
hyfedredd proficiency
hyfforddai trainee
hyfforddedig trained

hyfforddeion trainees
hyfforddi to coach, to instruct,
   to train
hyfforddiant instruction, training,
   tuition
hyfforddwr coach, instructor,
   trainer
hyfforddwyr instructors
hyfryd delightful, lovely, nice,
   pleasant
hyfrydwch delight, pleasure
hyfyw viable
hyfywedd viability
hygrededd credibility
hygyrch accessible
hygyrchedd accessibility
hylendid hygiene
hylif fluid, liquid
hylifau fluids
hyll hideous, ugly
hymateb response
hymchwil research
hymddygiad behaviour
hymdrechion efforts
hymestyn to reach, to stretch
hymgorffori personify
hymroddiad commitment
hymrwymiad commitment
hymweliad visit
hyn these, this
hŷn elder
hynaf elder, eldest
hynafiaid ancestors

hynafol ancient
hynna that
hynny that
hynod notable, noteworthy,
   remarkable
hynt course, way
hynysu to isolate
hyrddod rams
hyrwyddo to facilitate, to further,
   to promote
hysbryd spirit
hysbrydoli to inspire
hysbys evident, known, well-
   known
hysbyseb advertisement
hysbysebion advertisements,
   adverts
hysbysebu to advertise
hysbysiad announcement, notice
hysbysiadau announcements
hysbysir (is/will be) informed
hysbysodd (he/she/it) informed
hysbysu to inform, to notify
hysbyswyd (was) informed
hysgol[1] ladder
hysgol[2] school
hysgolion[1] ladders
hysgolion[2] schools
hysgrifennu to write
hystafell room
hystyried to consider
hytrach rather

I : i

i for, that, to
  i'ch for your, to your
  i'm for my, to my
  i'th for your, to your
  i'w[1] for their, to their
  i'w[2] for his/her
iâ ice
iach healthy, sound, wholesome
iachach healthier
iachawdwriaeth salvation
iachus bracing, healthy
iaith language, tongue
iâr hen
iard playground, yard
iarll count, earl
ias shiver, shudder, thrill
iau[1] younger
iau[2] liver
Iau[1] Thursday
Iau[2] Jupiter
iawn[1] very
iawn[2] all right, correct, ok, right
iawn[3] atonement, compensation
iawndal compensation, damages
iawnderau rights
ichi for you, that you, to you
ichwi for you, that you, to you
id id
Iddew Jew
Iddewig Jewish
Iddewon Jews
iddi for her, to her, that she
iddo for him, to him, that he

iddo'i for he him, that he him, to he him
iddyn for them, to them, that they
iddynt for them, to them, that they
ie yes, yea
iechyd health, heavens!
ieir chickens
ieithoedd languages
ieithyddol linguistic
Iesu Jesus
ieuainc young
ieuanc young
ieuenctid youth
ieuengaf youngest
ifainc young
ifanc juvenile, young
ig hiccup
ildio to surrender, to yield
ill the {...} of them
im for me, to me, that I
imi for me, to me, that I
inc ink
incwm income
indecs index
Indiad Indian
Indiaid Indians
Indiaidd Indian
ing anguish, distress
injan engine
innau I, myself
inni for us, to us, that we
integredig integrated

integreiddio to integrate
iogwrt yoghurt
Ionawr January
ir fresh, juicy, succulent
is below, beneath, lower
isadeiledd infrastructure
isadran subsection
isaf lowest, nethermost
isafon tributary
isafonydd tributaries
isafswm minimum
is-baragraff sub-paragraph
is-bwyllgor sub-committee
is-ddeddf by-law

is-ddeddfau by-laws
isel depressed, low, menial
iselder depression, lowness
iseldir lowland
iseldiroedd lowlands
is-gadeirydd vice-chairman
is-ganghellor vice-chancellor
isio to want
islaw[1] below, underneath
islaw[2] below, beneath
isod below
israddedig undergraduate
israddedigion undergraduates
iti for you, to you, that you

J : j

jac jack
jam jam
jeli jelly

job job
jôc joke
jyst just

L : l

a word starting with l printed in *italics* means that the root form
of that word begins with **ll**, e.g. *ladd* root **lladd;**
or with **g**, e.g. *lân* root **glân**

in a Welsh dictionary, unlike this list, **ll** is a letter in its own right and
follows *ly* and precedes *m* alphabetically

label label
labeli labels
labelu to label
labordai laboratories
labordy laboratory
lach lash
ladd to kill
laddodd (he/she/it) killed
laddwyd (was) killed
laeth milk
lafar vocal
lafur labour
lai less
lais voice
lamp lamp
lampau lamps
lan[1] up
lan[2] bank, side
lan[3] church
lân[1] clean, fair, holy
lân[2] utter, complete
lanc youth
landlord landlord
landlordiaid landlords
lanhau to clean
lanio to land
lannau[1] banks

lannau[2] church
lansiad launch
lansio to launch
lansiodd (he/she/it) launched
lansiwyd (was) launched
lanw[1] to fill
lanw[2] tide
lapio to swaddle, to wrap
larwm alarm
larymau alarms
las blue
laser laser
last shoe-last
laswellt grass
law[1] hand, handwriting, side, care
law[2] rain
lawdriniaeth surgery
lawenydd happiness
lawer many
lawn full
lawnt green, lawn
lawr[1] down
lawr[2] laver
lawr[3] floor, storey
lawysgrifau manuscripts
le place
lechi slates

led¹ fairly
led² breadth
ledaenu to spread
leddfu to ease
ledled throughout
lefaru to speak
lefel level
lefelau levels
lefydd places
leiaf least
leiafrifoedd minorities
leiafrifol minority
leihad reduction
leihau to reduce
lein line, line-out
leisio to voice
lem acute
lên literature
lenorion literary figures
lens lens
lenwi to fill
lenyddiaeth literature
lenyddol literary
leoedd places
leol local
leoli to place
leoliad location
leoliadau locations
leolir (is/will be) located
les benefit, welfare
lestri dishes
lethr slope
lethrau slopes
lety lodging
lew¹ lion
lew² bold, courageous
li current, flood, flow

licio to like
lid anger, inflammation
lif flood
lifft elevator, lift
lifo to flow
lifogydd floods
lifrai livery, uniform
limrig limerick
linc link
linell line, line-out
linellau lines
liniaru to ease
litr litre
liw¹ colour
liw² by
liwiau colours
liwt lute
llac lax, loose, slack
llach lash
llachar brilliant, dazzling, glittering
lladd to kill, to relieve, to slay
lladdodd (he/she/it) killed
lladdwyd (was) killed
Lladin Latin
lladron thieves
llaeth milk
llafar oral, vocal, vociferous
llafn blade, lad
llafur¹ labour, toil
llafur² corn
llafurus arduous, hard, laborious
llai¹ fewer, lesser, smaller
llai² less, minus
llaid mud
llain plot (of land), strip, wicket
llais voice, say
llaith damp, moist

llall (the) other, (the) second
llamu to jump, to leap, to spring
llan church
llanast mess
llanc lad, young man, youth
llannau churchyards, churches
llanw[1] flood tide, influx, tide
llanw[2] filling, relief
llanw[3] to fill
llath yard
llaw hand, handwriting, side
llawdriniaeth operation
llawen happy, jovial, merry
llawenydd happiness, joy, merriment
llawer[1] great deal, lot, many, much
llawer[2] far, lot, much
llawfeddyg surgeon
llawfeddygol surgical
llawlyfr handbook, manual
llawn[1] complete, entire, full
llawn[2] a bit, just as, rather
llawnach fuller
llawnamser full-time
llawr floor, storey
llawysgrif manuscript
llawysgrifau manuscripts
lle[1] place, room, space
lle[2] where
llech flag, slate, stone
llechen slate
llechi slates
llechu to hide, to lurk, to shelter
llecyn spot
llecynnau places
lled[1] breadth, width

lled[2] fairly, partly, semi-
lledaeniad dissemination
lledaenu to disseminate, to spread
lleddfu to alleviate, to ease, to soothe
lledr leather
lledu to broaden, to spread out, to widen
llef cry, shout, wail
llefaru to speak, to utter
llefarydd spokesman, spokesperson
lleferydd speech, utterance
llefrith milk
llefydd places
lleia' least, lesser, smallest, youngest
lleiaf least, lesser, smallest, youngest
lleiafrif minority
lleiafrifoedd minorities
lleiafrifol minority
lleiafswm minimum
lleidr burglar, robber, thief
lleied so few, so little, so small
lleihad decrease, reduction
lleihau to decrease, to lessen, to reduce
lleill others
lleiniau strips of land
lleisiau voices
lleisio to express, to sing, to voice
lleithder dampness, humidity, moisture
llem acute

llen curtain, veil
llên literature
lleng host, legion, multitude
llenni curtains
llenor author
llenorion literary figures
llenwch (you) fill
llenwi to fill
llenyddiaeth literature
llenyddol literary
lleoedd places
lleol local
lleoli to locate, to place
lleoliad location, position
lleoliadau locations
lleolir (is/will be) located
lles benefit, good, welfare
llesol advantageous, beneficial,
    salutary
llesteirio to hinder, to impede,
    to obstruct
llestri crockery, dishes
llethol overpowering,
    overwhelming
llethr hillside, slope
llethrau slopes
llety accommodation, inn, lodging
lletya to accommodate,
    to house, to lodge
lleuad moon, the Moon
llew lion
llewod lions
llewyrch brightness, prosperity,
    radiance, sheen, success
llewyrchus flourishing, thriving
lleyg lay
lli current, flood, flow

lliain cloth, linen, tablecloth, towel
lliaws host, multitude
llid anger, fury, inflammation, ire,
    irritation, wrath
llif¹ current, flow
llif² saw
llifanu to grind, to hone, to whet
llifio to saw
llifo to flow
llifogydd floods
llinell boundary, crease, line,
    queue, row, stripe
llinellau lines
lliniarol mitigating, soothing
lliniaru to alleviate, to ease, to
    soothe
llinyn line, sinew, string, thread,
    twine
llithro to glide, to slide, to slip
lliw¹ colour
lliw² coloured
lliwgar colourful, vivid
lliwiau colours
lliwio to colour, to dye
llo calf (cow), oaf
lloches refuge, shelter
Lloegr England
lloer moon
lloeren satellite
llofft bedroom, upstairs
llofnod autograph, signature
llofnodi to sign
llofnodwyd (was) autographed,
    signed
llofrudd murderer
llofruddiaeth murder
llog interest

llogi to hire, to lease
lloi calves (cows)
llon cheerful, happy, jolly, joyful
llond full
llong ship
llongau ships
llongyfarch to compliment,
  to congratulate
llongyfarchiad congratulation
llongyfarchiadau
  congratulations
llonydd quiet, still, tranquil
lloriau floors
llorweddol horizontal
llosg burning
llosgi to burn, to shine
llu host, throng
lludw ash
llun drawing, form, photograph,
  picture, shape
Llun Monday
Llundain London
llungopïo to photocopy
lluniaeth fare, food, sustenance
lluniau pictures
llunio to construct, to design,
  to fashion, to form
lluniwch (you) design, form
lluniwyd (was) designed, formed
lluoedd forces
lluosi to multiply
lluosog plural
llusgo to drag
llw curse, oath, vow
llwch[1] dust, fertiliser
llwch[2] inlet, loch
llwm bare, barren, bleak, poor

llwy spoon
llwybr path, way
llwybrau paths
llwyd brown, grey, holy, pale, wan
llwyddiannau successes
llwyddiannus successful
llwyddiant success
llwyddo to succeed
llwyddodd (he/she/it) succeeded
llwyddwyd (was) succeeded
llwyfan stage, dais, rostrum
llwyn bush, grove, thicket
llwyni thickets
llwynog fox
llwyr complete, total, utter
llwyth[1] burden, load
llwyth[2] tribe
llwythau tribes
llwythi burdens
llwytho to load
llydan broad, wide
llydanddail broad-leaved
Llydaw Brittany
Llydaweg Breton
llyfn even, level, smooth
llyfr book
llyfrau books
llyfrfa library, publisher
llyfrgell library
llyfrgelloedd libraries
llyfrgellydd librarian
llyfryddiaeth bibliography
llyfryn booklet, pamphlet
llyfrynnau booklets
llyg shrew
llygad eye, source
llygaid eyes

llygod mice
llygoden mouse
llygredd corruption, depravity, pollution
llygredig corrupt, degraded
llygru to contaminate, to corrupt, to pollute
llym harsh, rigorous, severe, sharp, strict
llyn lake
llyncu to absorb, to swallow
llynedd last year
llynges fleet, navy
llynnoedd lakes
llys[1] court, hall
llys[2] slime
llysiau herbs, plants, vegetables
llysoedd courts
llystyfiant vegetation
llythrennau letters (alphabet)
llythrennedd literacy
llythrennol literal
llythyr epistle, letter
llythyrau letters (correspondence)
llythyren letter (alphabet)
llythyron letters (correspondence)
llyw helm, rudder, steering-wheel
llywio to pilot, to steer
llywodraeth government
llywodraethau governments
llywodraethol governing, ruling
llywodraethu to control, to govern, to rule
llywodraethwr governor
llywodraethwyr governors

llywydd dominant (music), president
lo[1] coal
lo[2] calf (cow)
lobïo to lobby
loches shelter
loes pain
lofaol mining
lofnodi to sign
log interest, log
logi to hire
logio to log
logisteg logistics
lolfa lounge, sitting-room
lon happy
lôn lane
lond full of
long ship
longau ships
lonydd quiet
lorïau lorries
lorri lorry
losgi to burn
lot lot
loteri lottery
lu host
lun drawing, photograph, picture
luniau pictures
lunio to formulate
luniwyd (was) designed, formed
luoedd forces
lusgo to drag
lw oath
lwc luck
lwch dust
lwcus lucky
lwfans allowance

lwfansau allowances
lwybr path
lwybrau paths
lwyd grey
lwyddiannus successful
lwyddiant success
lwyddo to succeed
lwyddodd (he/she/it) succeeded
lwyfan stage
lwyr complete
lwyth[1] load
lwyth[1] tribe
lwytho to load
lydan wide
lyfr book
lyfrau books
lyfrgell library
lyfrgelloedd libraries
lyfryn booklet
lygad eye
lygaid eyes

lygredd corruption
lygru to corrupt, to pollute
lyn[1] valley
lyn[2] lake
lŷn (he/she/it) sticks
lyncu to swallow
lynu to stick
lys court
lysiau vegetables
lysoedd courts
lystyfiant vegetation
lythrennau letters (alphabet)
lythyr letter (correspondence)
lythyrau letters (correspondence)
lythyren letter (alphabet)
lywio to steer
lywodraeth government
lywodraethol ruling
lywodraethu to rule
lywodraethwyr governor
lywydd president

M : m

a word starting with **m** printed in *italics* means that the root form
of that word begins with **b**, e.g. *mlwyddyn* root **blwyddyn**;
a word starting with **mh** printed in *italics* means that the root form
of that word begins with **p**, e.g. *mhlentyn* root **plentyn**

mab son, boy
mabwysiadu to adopt
mabwysiadwyd (was) adopted
machlud[1] sunset
machlud[2] to go down, to set
madarch mushrooms, toadstools
maddau to forgive, to pardon
maddeuant forgiveness, pardon
mae[1] is/are
   mae'ch your {...} is/are
mae[2] bay
maen[1] griddle, stone
maen[2] (they) are
maenor manor
maent (they) are
maer mayor
maes[1] area, field, ground
maes[2] out
maeth[1] nourishment
maeth[2] foster
maethiad nutrition
maetholion nutrients
maetholyn nutrient
maethu to foster
magnetig magnetic
magu to rear, to raise, to nurse, to breed
magwyd (was) reared, raised, nursed

mai[1] that, that it (is)
mai[2] blame, falut
Mai may
main thin
mainc bench
maint extent, number, quantity, size
Mair Mary
maith long, tedious
malu to break, to grind, to shatter, to smash
malwod snails
mam mother
mamaliaid mammals
mamau mothers
mam-gu grandmother
mami mammy
mamiaith mother tongue
mamog in-lamb ewe
mamogiaid ewes
mamolaeth maternity, motherhood
man place, spot
mân fine, little, petty, small, trifling
mangre district, place, premises
mannau places
mantais advantage
manteisio to exploit, to take advantage (of)

manteisiol advantageous
manteision advantages
mantell cape, cloak, mantle
mantol balance
mantolen balance-sheet
manwerthu to retail
manwl detailed, exact, precise
manylach more detailed
manylder detail, precision
manyleb specification
manylebau specifications
manylion details
manylrwydd detail, precision
manylu to detail, to go into
    details
map map
mapiau maps
mapio to map
marc mark
march stallion, steed
marchnad market
marchnadoedd markets
marchnata to market,
    to promote
marchogaeth to ride
marciau marks
marcio to mark
marn judgement, opinion
marw[1] to die
marw[2] dead, deceased, lifeless
marwol deadly, fatal, lethal,
    mortal
marwolaeth death, mortality
marwolaethau deaths
marwoldeb mortality
mas[1] out
mas[2] bass

màs mass
masnach trade
masnachol commercial,
    mercantile
masnachu to trade
masnachwr dealer, merchant,
    trader
masnachwyr traders
mater matter, subject, topic
materion matters
materol material, materialistic
math[1] kind, sort, type
math[2] such
màth bath
mathau sorts
mathemateg mathematics
mathemategol mathematical
matryd to undress
maw dirt
mawl praise, worship
mawn peat
mawr big, great, important, large,
    much
mawredd grandeur, greatness
mawreddog boastful, grand,
    pompous
mawrhydi majesty
mawrion big, prominent
    people
Mawrth[1] Tuesday
Mawrth[2] March
Mawrth[3] Mars
mebyd childhood, youth
mecanwaith mechanism
mecanweithiau mechanisms
mecanyddol mechanical
medal medal

medd¹ mead
medd² (he/she/it) says
medd³ grave
medda (I/I will) say
meddaf (I/I will) say
meddai (he/she/it would/ used to) say
meddal soft, tender
meddalwedd software
medden (they would/used to) say
meddiannu to occupy, to possess, to take possession of
meddiannydd occupant, owner
meddiant occupation, possession
meddu to own, to possess, to take possession of
meddwi to get drunk, to intoxicate
meddwl¹ idea, mind, thought
meddwl² to intend, to mean, to think
meddwn¹ (I would/used to) say
meddwn² (we/we will) say
meddyg doctor, physician
meddygaeth medicine
meddygfa surgery
meddygfeydd surgeries
meddyginiaeth medication, remedy
meddyginiaethau remedies
meddygol medical
meddygon doctors
meddylfryd disposition, mentality
meddyliau thoughts
meddyliodd (he/she/it) thought
meddyliol mental

meddyliwch (you) think
medi to reap
Medi September
medr ability, capacity, skill
medra (he/she/it is) able
medrai (he/she/it would/ used to) be able
medrau abilities, gifts
medrir (is/will be) able
medru to be able, to know
medrus clever, expert, skilful
medrusrwydd prowess
medrwch (you) are able, can
medrwn¹ (we are/will be) able
medrwn² (I would/used to) be able
megis as, like
Mehefin June
meibion sons
meic bike
meillion clover
meillionen clover
meincnodi to benchmark
meinhau to taper
meini stones
meintiau sizes
meintiol quantitative
meinwe gauze, tissue
meirch stallions
meirw dead
meistr boss, master
meistri masters
meithrin to cultivate, to nourish, to rear
meithrinfa crèche, nursery
mêl honey
melen yellow

melin mill
melinau mills
mellt lightning
mellten lightning
melyn yellow
melys sweet
memorandwm memorandum
menig gloves
menter risk, speculation, venture
mentor mentor
mentora to mentor
mentoriaid mentors
mentrau ventures
mentro to dare, to risk, to venture
mentrus daring, enterprising,
   risky, venturesome
menyn butter
menyw female, woman
menywod women
merch daughter, girl
merched girls
Mercher[1] Wednesday
Mercher[2] Mercury
Meseia Messiah
mesul by
mesur[1] bill, measure,
   measurement
mesur[2] to measure
mesuradwy measurable
mesurau measures
mesuriad measurement
mesuriadau measurements
mesurydd meter
mesuryddion meters
metel metal
metelau metals
methdaliad bankruptcy

methiannau failures
methiant failure
methodd (he/she/it) failed
Methodist Methodist
Methodistiaid Methodists
methodoleg methodology
methu to fail, to miss
metr metre
metrig metric
mewn in
mewnbwn input
mewndirol inland
mewnforio to import
mewnforion imports
mewnfudiad immigration
mewnfudo to immigrate
mewnfudwr immigrant, incomer
mewnfudwyr immigrants
mewnlifiad influx
mewnol inner, inside, internal
mewnrwyd intranet
meysydd fields
mha which
mhanel panel
mharagraff paragraph
mharagraffau paragraphs
mharc park
mhell far
mhen head
mhennod chapter
mhentref village
mhlas mansion
mhlentyn child
mhlith amid
mhlwyf parish
mhob every
mhobman everywhere

mhresenoldeb presence
mhrif chief, main
mhrifysgol university
mhrofiad experience
mi¹ I, me
mi² {*introduces a statement*}
mil thousand
mileniwm millennium
milfeddygol veterinary
miliwn million
miliynau millions
milltir mile
milltiroedd miles
miloedd thousands
milwr soldier
milwrol martial, military
milwyr soldiers
min edge, point, verge
miniog sharp, pointed,
    penetrating
minnau myself
minne myself
mis month
misoedd months
misol monthly
miwsig music
mlaen front
mlaenau fronts
mlwch box
mlwydd year
mlwyddyn year
mlychau boxes
mlynedd years
mlynyddoedd years
mo no, not
    mo'i not his/her/its
    mo'u not their

moch¹ pigs
moch² cheek
mochyn pig, swine
mod¹ am
mod² that
modd¹ means, way
modd² mode, mood
modd³ contentedness, pleasure
moddion medicine
model model
modelau models
modelu to model
modern modern
moderneiddio to modernise
modfedd inch
modiwl module
modiwlau modules
modrwy ring
modryb aunt
modur automobile, motor,
    motor car
modurdy garage
moduron cars
moel¹ bald, bare, plain
moel² hilltop
moesegol ethical
moesol moral
moethus luxurious, sumptuous
'mofyn to fetch, to want
mohono not him/it
mol belly
molchi to wash (oneself)
molysgiaid molluscs
moment moment
môn base, root
Môn Anglesey
monitro to monitor

mor as, how, so
môr sea
mordaith cruise, voyage
mordwyo to navigate, to sail
more early, morning
morfa fen, salt-marsh
morfil whale
morfilod whales
morgais mortgage
morglawdd breakwater, dyke, embankment
moroedd seas
morol marine, maritime
morwr mariner, sailor, seaman
morwrol maritime
morwyn maid, virgin
morwyr seamen
mrawd brother
mro region, vale
mron breast
mud dumb, mute, speechless
mudiad movement
mudiadau movements
mudo to migrate, to move
mudol migrant, migratory
mul donkey, mule
munud minute
munudau minutes
mur wall
muriau walls
musnes business
mwd mud
mwg fumes, smoke
mwmian to mumble
mwrdeistref borough
mwy¹ bigger, further, greater, more
mwy² again, any more

mwya' greatest, largest, most
mwyach any more, henceforth
mwyaf greatest, largest, most, major
mwyafrif majority, preponderance
mwyfwy increasingly, more and more
mwyn¹ mineral, ore
mwyn² in order
mwyn³ gentle, mild, tender
mwynau minerals
mwynderau delights, pleasures
mwynglawdd mine
mwyngloddiau mines
mwyngloddio to mine
mwynhad enjoyment, pleasure
mwynhau to enjoy
myd world
myfi it is I, myself
myfyrdod contemplation, meditation
myfyrio to contemplate, to meditate, to ponder
myfyriwr student
myfyrwraig student (female)
myfyrwyr students
mygu to smoke, to steam, to suffocate
mymryn bit, mite, particle
myn¹ kid
myn² by
myn³ (he/she/it) insists
mynach friar, monk
mynachod monks
mynd¹ to go, to depart, to travel, to take, to become

mynd² go, zip
myned to go, to depart, to travel, to take, to become
mynedfa entrance, gateway
mynedfeydd entrances
mynediad access, admission
mynegai index
mynegeio to index
mynegeion indexes, indices
mynegi to express, to indicate
mynegiant expression
mynegir (is/will be) expressed
mynegodd (he/she/it) expressed
mynegwyd (was) expressed
mynnai (he/she/it would/ used to) insist
mynnir (is/will be) insisted
mynnodd (he/she/it) insisted

mynnu to insist, to persist, to wish
mynnwch (you) insist
mynwent cemetery, graveyard
mynwentydd cemeteries
mynwes bosom, breast
mynych frequent
mynychaf most frequent
mynychder frequency, prevalence, repetition
mynychu to attend, to frequent, to visit regularly
mynydd mountain
mynyddig mountainous
mynyddoedd mountains
mysg midst
mywyd life

N : n

a word starting with **n** printed in *italics* means that the root form
of that word begins with **d**, e.g. *ninas* root **dinas**;
a word starting with **ng** printed in *italics* means that the root form
of that word begins with **g**, e.g. *ngeiriau* root **geiriau**;
a word starting with **ngh** printed in *italics* means that the root form
of that word begins with **c**, e.g. *nghwpan* root **cwpan**;
a word starting with **nh** printed in *italics* means that the root form
of that word begins with **t**, e.g. *nhad* root **tad**

in a Welsh dictionary, unlike this list, **ng** is a letter in its own right and
follows *gy* (not *ny*) and precedes *h* alphabetically

---

na[1] no, not
na[2] neither, nor
   na'i[1] nor his/her/its
   na'u[1] nor their
   na'r[1] nor the
na[3] that {...} not, which {...} not,
  whom {...} not, who {...} not
na[4] than
   na'i[2] than his/her/its
   na'r[2] than the
   na'u[2] than their
nabod to know
nac no, not
nad no, not
naddo no
naddu to carve, to chip
Nadolig Christmas
nag than
nage no
nai nephew
naid[1] jump, leap
naid[2] (he/she/it) jumps

naill either ... (or), the one ...
  (the other[s])
nain grandma, grandmother
nam blemish, defect, fault
namau faults
namyn except, minus
nant[1] brook, stream
nant[2] tooth
naratif narrative
nas no, not
natblygiad development
natur nature, temper
naturiol innate, natural
naw nine
nawdd patronage, sponsorship,
  support
nawfed ninth
nawr now
naws feel, tinge, touch
ne[1] south
ne[2] right
neb anyone, nobody, no one

nedd adze, axe
neddf act, law, statute
nef bliss, heaven
nefoedd heaven
nefol celestial, heavenly
negatif negative
neges errand, message
negeseuon messages
negodi to negotiate
negyddol negative
neidio to jump, to pounce,
   to vault
neidiodd (he/she/it) jumped
neidr snake
Neifion Neptune
neilltu one side
neilltuo to reserve, to seclude,
   to set to one side
neilltuol particular, special
neilltuwyd (was) reserved
neis nice
neithiwr last night
nen ceiling, sky, the heavens
nenfwd ceiling
neno heavens!
nentydd streams
nepell near
nerfol nervous
nerfus nervous, nervy,
   anxious
nerth power, strength, vigour
nerthol mighty, strong
nes¹ nearer
nes² till, until
nesa next
nesaf next, nearest
net net

neu or, or else
   neu'ch or your
   neu'i or his/her/its
neuadd hall
neuaddau halls
newid¹ change
newid² to alter, to change,
   to exchange
newidiadau changes
newidiodd (he/she/it) changed
newidiol changeable
newidiwyd (was) changed
newydd¹ news
newydd² new
newydd³ just, recently
newyddiaduraeth journalism
newyddiadurwr journalist
newyddiadurwyr journalists
newyddion news, new
newyddlen news sheet
newyn famine, starvation
newynog hungry
ngair word
ngeiriau words
ngeni to be born
nghaer fort
nghalon heart
nghanllaw guideline, rail
nghanol middle
nghanolbarth midland
nghanolfan centre
nghap cap
nghapel chapel
ngharchar jail
nghariad love
nghartref home
nghastell castle

nghefn back
ngheg mouth
ngholeg college
ngholofn column
nghorff body
nghwm valley
nghwmni company
nghwpan cup
nghwrs course
nghyd joint
nghyd-destun context
nghyfarfod meeting
nghyfarfodydd meetings
nghyffiniau vicinity
nghyfnod period
nghyfraith law
nghyfres series
Nghymru Wales
nghynllun plan
nghynulliad assembly
nghysgod shadow
nghystadleuaeth competition
nghyswllt context
ngofal care
ngogledd north
ngoleuni light
ngolwg view
Ngorffennaf July
ngorllewin west
ngwaelod bottom
ngwaith work
ngweddill remainder
ngwely bed
ngwendid weakness
ngwlad country
ngwledydd countries
ngwres heat

nhabl table
nhad father
nhad-cu grandfather
nhaid grandfather
nhermau terms
nheulu family
nhîm team
nhraed feet
nhref town
nhrefn order
nhrwyn nose
nhw them
nhyb opinion
nhymor season, term
ni[1] us, we
ni[2] not
nid not
nifer number
niferoedd numbers
niferus numerous
ninnau ourselves
nis not
nitrogen nitrogen
niwclear nuclear
niwed damage, harm, hurt
niwedd end
niweidio to damage, to harm, to hurt
niweidiol detrimental, harmful
niwl fog, haze, mist
niwmismateg numismatics
niwrnod day
niwsans nuisance
niwtral neutral
nod[1] aim, brand, objective
nod[2] node
nodau notes

noddedig sponsored
noddfa refuge, sanctuary, shelter
noddi to patronise, to sponsor
noddir (is/will be) sponsored
noddwr patron, sponsor
noddwyd (was) sponsored
noddwyr sponsors
nodedig notable, remarkable
noder (let it be) noted
nodi[1] to mark, to note
nodi[2] to plant, to put
nodiadau notes
nodir (is/will be) noted
nododd (he/she/it) noted
nodwch (you) note
nodwedd characteristic, feature, trait
nodweddiadol characteristic, typical
nodweddion characteristics
nodweddu to typify
nodwyd (was) noted
nodwydd needle
nodyn note
noeth bare, bare-faced, naked
nofel novel

nofelau novels
nofelydd novelist
nofio to swim
nôl to bring, to fetch
Normanaidd Norman
Normaniad Norman
Normaniaid Normans
nos night
noson evening, night
noswaith evening, night
nosweithiau nights
Nuw God
nwy[1] gas
nwy[2] two
nwyddau goods, ware
nwylo hands
nwyon gases
nydd day
nyddiau days
nyffryn vale, valley
nyrs nurse
nyrsio to nurse
nyrsys nurses
nyth nest
nythod nests
nythu to nest, to nestle

O : o

---

a word starting with **o** printed in *italics* means that the root form
of that word begins with **g**, e.g. *obaith* root **gobaith**

---

o¹ by, from, of
  o'ch from your, of your
  o'i from his/her/its, of his/
  her/its
  o'm from my, of my
  o'th from your, of your
  o'u from their, of their
o² he, him, it
o³ oh!
obaith hope
obeithio to hope
obeithiol hopeful
oblegid because, on account of,
  owing to
oblygiadau implications
oc AD
och oh!
ochor side
ochr side, edge, aspect
ochrau sides
ocsigen oxygen
od odd, strange
oddef to suffer
oddeutu about, approximately
oddi from, out of
oddieithr except, unless
odid hardly, scarcely
odidog excellent
odl rhyme
odli to rhyme
odyn¹ kiln

odyn² (they) are, are (they)?
oed age
oedd was, were
oeddan (they) were
oeddech (you) were
oeddem (we) were
oedden (they) were
oeddent (they) were
oeddwn (I) was
oeddynt (they) were
oedfa meeting, service
oedi to delay, to linger, to wait
oedolion adults
oedolyn adult
oedran age
oedrannus aged, elderly
oen lamb
oer cold
oerfel cold
oergell fridge, refrigerator
oeri to chill, to get cold
oerni cold
oes¹ age, era, lifetime
oes² (is/are) there?
oes³ yes
oesau ages
oesoedd ages
oesol perpetual
of blacksmith
ofal care
ofalu to care

ofalus careful
ofalwyr carers, caretakers
ofer futile, vain, wasteful
offeiriad parson, priest
offeiriaid priests
offer implements
offeryn implement, instrument, tool
offerynnau instruments
offrwm offering, sacrifice
ofid worry
ofn dread, fear, trepidation
ofnadwy awful, terrible
ofnau fears
ofni to be afraid, to fear, to regret
ofnus fearful, nervous, timid
ofod space
ofyn to ask
ofyniad question
ofynion requirements
ofynnir (is/will be) asked
ofynnodd (he/she/it) asked
ofynnol required
ofynnwyd (was) asked
oglau scents, smells
ogledd north
ogleddol northern
ogof cave, grotto
ogoniant splendour
ogystal as well as
ohebiaeth correspondence
oherwydd because
ohirio to postpone
ohoni from her/it, of her/it
ohono from him/it, of him/it
ohonoch from you, of you
ohonom from us, of us

ohonon from us, of us
ohonyn from them, of them
ohonynt from them, of them
ôl[1] impression, mark, track
ôl[2] behind, rear
ola' final, last
olaf final, last
olau light
olchi to wash
oleuadau lights
oleuni light
oleuo to light
olew oil
olion tracks
oll all, (not) at all
ollwng to release
ollyngiadau releases
ôl-raddedig post-graduate
olrhain to follow, to plot, to trace
olwg look, sight
olwyn wheel
olwynion wheels
olygfa view
olygfeydd sights, views
olygir[1] (is/will be) meant
olygir[2] (is/will be) edited
olygu[1] to mean
olygu[2] to edit
olygydd editor
olygyddion editors
Olympaidd Olympic
olyniaeth succession
olynol consecutive, successive
olynydd successor
ombwdsman ombudsman
ombwdsmon ombudsman

ond but, only
onest honest
onestrwydd honesty
ongl angle
onglau angles
oni unless
onid is it not?, isn't it?
opera opera
opsiwn option
opsiynau options
optegol optical
orau best
orchmynion commands
orchudd cover
orchuddio to cover
orchwyl task
orchymyn command,
  commandment
ordnans ordnance
oren orange
oresgyn to defeat
orffen to complete
Orffennaf July
orffwys to rest
orffwysfa caesura, resting place
orfod to have to
orfodaeth compulsion
orfodi to force
orfodol compulsory
organ organ
organau organs

organeb organism
organebau organisms
organeddau organisms
organig organic
oriau hours
oriel gallery
orielau galleries
orlawn overflowing
orllewin west
orllewinol western
ormod too much
ormodol to excess
ornest contest
oroesi to survive
orsaf station
orsafoedd stations
orsedd throne
oruchwyliaeth supervision
oruchwylio to supervise
orwedd to lie
os if
osgo posture, slant, slope, stance
osgoi to avoid, to elude
osod to set
osodir (is/will be) set
osododd (he/she/it) set
osodwyd (was) set
osôn ozone
ostwng to lower
ostyngiad reduction
ots care, matter

P : p

a word starting with **ph** printed in *italics* means that the root form
of that word begins with **p**, e.g. *phapur* root **papur**

p'un which one
pa how, what, when, which
Pab Pope
pabell tent, pavilion, marquee
pac kit, pack
pacio to pack
paent paint
pafiliwn pavilion
paham wherefore, why
paid (you) don't!
paith pampas, prairie, range
palas palace
palmant pavement
pam why
pan¹ when, while
pan² pan
paned cup of
panel panel
paneli panels
pant depression, dip, valley
papur paper
papurau papers
pâr¹ pair
pâr² (he/she/it) causes
para to last
paragraff paragraph
paragraffau paragraphs
paratoad preparation
paratoadau preparations
paratoi to groom, to prepare
paratowyd (was) prepared

parau pairs
parc field, park
parch esteem, respect, veneration
parchedig reverend
Parchg Rev.
parchu to respect, to revere,
  to venerate
parchus respectable, respectful
parciau parks
parcio to park
parhad continuation, durability,
  sequel, wear
parhaodd (he/she/it) lasted
parhaol durable, permanent
parhau to last, to continue,
  to prolong
parhaus continual, sustained
parlwr parlour
parod obliging, ready, take-away,
  willing
parodrwydd readiness
parsel parcel
parth district, domain, part
parthau parts
parthed concerning, regarding
parti fête, party
partïon parties
partner mate, partner
partneriaeth partnership
partneriaethau partnerships
partneriaid partners

pasbort passport
pasbortau passports
Pasg Easter
pasio to pass
patrwm example, pattern
patrymau patterns
pawb everybody
pe if
pebyll tents
pechod sin
pechodau sins
pecyn pack, package
pecynnau packages
pecynnu to package
pedair four
pedol horseshoe
pedwar four
pedwaredd fourth
pedwerydd fourth
peidio to cease, to refrain
peidiwch (you) don't!
peilot pilot
peint pint
peintio to paint
peiriannau engines, machines
peirianneg engineering
peiriannwr engineer, mechanic
peiriant engine, machine
peirianwaith machinery,
    mechanism
peirianwyr engineers, mechanics
peirianyddol mechanical
pêl ball
pêl-droed football, soccer
pêl-droediwr footballer, soccer
    player
pelen ball, pellet

peli balls
pell distant, far, long
pellach[1] further, later
pellach[2] any longer
pellaf furthest
pelled as far as
pellter distance
pelydr rays
pelydryn beam, gleam, ray
pen end, head, top, chief, mouth
penaethiaid heads
penawdau headlines
pen-blwydd birthday
pencadlys headquarters
pencampwriaeth
    championship
pendant definite, positive
penderfynais (I) decided
penderfyniad decision,
    determination
penderfyniadau decisions
penderfynir (is/will be) decided
penderfynodd (he/she/it)
    decided
penderfynol determined,
    resolute
penderfynu to decide
penderfynwch (you) decide
penderfynwyd (was) decided
penillion verses
pennaeth chief, head
pennaf chief, predominant,
    principal
pennau heads
pennawd caption, heading
pennill stanza, verse
pennir (is/will be) specified

pennod chapter, episode
pennu to specify, to determine
pennwyd (was) specified
penodau chapters
penodedig appointed, determined, fixed
penodi to appoint
penodiad appointment
penodiadau appointments
penodir (is/will be) appointed
penodol distinct, especial, specific
penodwyd (was) appointed
pensaer architect
pensaernïaeth architecture
pensaernïol architectural
pensiwn pension
pensiynau pensions
pensiynwr pensioner, senior citizen
pensiynwyr pensioners
pentir headland
pentre' village
pentref village
pentrefi villages
pentwr heap, pile, stack
penwythnos weekend
perchen owner
perchennog owner, proprietor
perchenogaeth possession
perchenogion owners
pererin pilgrim
pererindod pilgrimage
perffaith perfect
perfformiad performance
perfformiadau performances
perfformio to perform
peri to cause, to induce

periglor incumbent, parson
persbectif perspective
person[1] person
person[2] parson
personau[1] persons
personau[2] parsons
personél personnel
personol personal
personoliaeth personality
perswadio to persuade
perth bush, hedge
perthi hedges
perthnasau relatives
perthnasedd relativity, relevance
perthnasol pertinent, relevant
perthyn to belong, to be related
perthynai (he/she/it would/ used to) belong
perthynas[1] relation, relative
perthynas[2] connection, relationship
perthynol relative
perwyl purpose
peryg danger
perygl danger, jeopardy, peril
peryglon dangers
peryglu to endanger, to jeopardise
peryglus dangerous, perilous, risky
petaech if (you) were
petaent if (they) were
petai if (he/she/it) were
peth thing, some
pethau things
pethe things
petrol petrol
pha what, which

pham why
phan when
phant hollow
phapur paper
phapurau papers
pharagraff paragraph
pharagraffau paragraphs
pharatoi to prepare
pharc park
pharch respect
pharhad continuation
pharhau to continue
phartner partner
phartneriaethau partnerships
phartneriaid partners
phatrwm pattern
phatrymau patterns
phawb everybody
phe if
phedair four
phedwar four
pheidio to cease
pheidiwch (you) don't!
pheiriannau engines, machines
phen head
phenderfyniad decision
phenderfyniadau decisions
phenderfynodd (he/she/it)
   decided
phenderfynu to decide
phenderfynwyd (was) decided
phennaeth head
phennu to determine
phenodi to appoint
phensiynau pensions
phentref village
phentrefi villages

pherfformiad performance
pherfformio to perform
pheri to cause
pherson parson, person
phersonol personal
pherthnasau relatives
pherthnasol relevant
pherthynas relation
pheryglon dangers
pheth thing
phethau things
phlanhigion plants
phlant children
phlentyn child
phob every
phobl people
phoblogaeth population
phoen pain
phoeni to worry
pholisi policy
pholisïau policies
phopeth everything
phosibl possible
photensial potential
phreifat private
phren wood
phresenoldeb presence
phridd earth, soil
phrif main
phrifysgol university
phrifysgolion universities
phrin scarce
phriodol appropriate
phris price
phrisiau prices
phroblem problem
phroblemau problems

phroffesiynol professional
phrofi to prove, to test
phrofiad experience
phrofiadau experiences
phrofion tests
phroses process
phrosesau processes
phrosesu to process
phrosiect project
phrosiectau projects
phryd when
phryder worry
phryderon worries
phrynu to buy
phum five
phump five
phwdin pudding
phwerau powers
phwnc subject
phwrpas purpose
phwy who
phwyllgor committee
phwynt point
phwysau weight(s)
phwysig important
phwysigrwydd importance
phwyslais emphasis
phwyso to weigh
phyllau pits
phynciau subjects
physgod fish(es)
piano piano, pianoforte
pibell pipe, tube
pibellau pipes
picnic picnic
pig[1] beak, bill, point, prong, spike, spout

pig[2] touchy
pigo to choose, to select, to pick, to peck, to prick, to sting
pin[1] pen, pin
pin[2] pine
pinc[1] pink
pinc[2] chaffinch
pistasio pistachio
pla plague, pestilence, pest
plaen[1] clear, frank, plain
plaen[2] plane
plaid party
planed planet
planhigfa plantation
planhigion plants
planhigyn plant
planigfeydd plantations
plannu to plant
plant children
plas country house, mansion, palace
plastig plastic
plasty mansion
plât plate
platiau plates
pleidiau parties
pleidlais vote
pleidleisiau votes
pleidleisio to poll, to vote
plentyn child
plentyndod childhood
pleser pleasure
pleserus enjoyable, pleasant
plesio to please, to satisfy
plismon policeman
plismona to police
plith midst

plu feathers, flakes, flies
plwg plug
plwm[1] lead (metal)
plwm[2] leaden, plumb
Plwton Pluto
plwyf parish
plwyfi parishes
plygu to bend, to bow, to fold, to submit
plymio to dive, to plumb, to plummet, to plunge
pnawn afternoon
po the
pob[1] every, each, all
pob[2] baked
pobl people, folk
pobloedd peoples
poblogaeth population, populace
poblogaethau populations
poblogaidd popular
poblogrwydd popularity
pobman everywhere
pobol people
poced pocket
poen ache, nuisance, pain
poeni to bother, to fret, to nag, to pester, to provoke, to tease, to worry
poenus aching, painful, sore
poeth hot, spicy
polisi policy
polisïau policies
politicaidd political
pont bridge, arch
pontio to bridge, to span
pontydd bridges

pop pop
popeth everything
popty bakehouse, oven
porfa grass, pasture
porfeydd grasslands
pori to browse, to graze
portffolio portfolio
porth[1] door, lobby, porch
porth[2] harbour
porthi to feed
porthiant food, nourishment
porthladd harbour, port
porthladdoedd harbours
portread portrait, portrayal
portreadu to portray
porwr browser, grazer
posib possible
posibiliadau possibilities
posibilrwydd possibility
posibl feasible, possible
positif positive
post post
poster poster
posteri posters
postio to post
postiwyd (was) posted
postyn post
potel bottle
poteli bottles
potensial potential
praidd congregation, flock
prawf probation, proof, test, trial
pregeth sermon
pregethu to preach, to go on
pregethwr preacher
preifat private
preifatrwydd privacy

premiwm premium
pren[1] wood, timber, tree
pren[2] wooden
prentis apprentice
prentisiaeth apprenticeship
prentisiaethau apprenticeships
prentisiaid apprentices
pres brass, money
Presbyteraidd Presbyterian
presennol present
presenoldeb presence
presgripsiwn prescription
presgripsiynau prescriptions
preswyl boarding, residential
preswylio to dwell, to reside
preswylwyr dwellers, residents
preswylydd dweller, inhabitant,
   resident
pridd earth, soil
priddoedd soils
prif chief, head, main, prime
prifardd award-winning poet
prifathro headmaster, principal
prifddinas capital city,
   metropolis
priffordd highway, main road
priffyrdd highways
prifwyl National Eisteddfod
prifysgol university
prifysgolion universities
prin[1] deficient, few, rare, scarce
prin[2] hardly, scarcely, barely
prinder dearth, scarcity, shortage
print print
printiedig printed
printio to print
priod[1] married

priod[2] partner, spouse
priod[3] proper
priodas marriage, matrimony,
   wedding
priodasau marriages
priodasol marital, matrimonial
priodi to marry, to wed,
   to couple
priodol appropriate, proper,
   suitable
priodoli to ascribe, to attribute
priodwedd property
priodweddau properties
pris price
prisiad valuation
prisiau prices
prisio to price, to value
problem problem
problemau problems
profedigaeth bereavement,
   tribulation
proffesiwn profession
proffesiynau professions
proffesiynol professional
proffil profile
proffwyd prophet
profi to prove, to test,
   to experience, to try
profiad experience
profiadau experiences
profiadol experienced, veteran
profion tests
profwyd (was) experienced,
   proven
prosbectws prospectus
proses process
prosesau processes

prosesu to process
prosesydd processor
prosiect project
prosiectau projects
protein protein
protest protest
Protestannaidd Protestant
protestio to protest,
   to remonstrate
protocol protocol
protocolau protocols
pryd¹ when, time
pryd² complexion
pryd³ meal
Prydain Britain
prydau meals
pryddest poem
Prydeinig British
pryder anxiety, worry
pryderon worries
pryderu to fret, to worry
pryderus anxious, worried
prydferth beautiful, handsome
prydferthwch beauty
prydiau times
prydles lease
prydlon prompt, punctual
pryf fly, grub, insect
pryfed flies, insects
pryfyn insect, worm
prynhawn afternoon
pryniad purchase
prynu to buy, to purchase,
   to redeem
prynwch (you) buy
prynwr buyer, consumer,
   redeemer

prynwyr buyers
prysur busy
prysurdeb busyness
pum five
pum deg fifty
pumdegau fifties
pumed fifth
pump five
punnau pounds
punnoedd pounds
punt pound
pur¹ pure
pur² fairly, quite
pwdin pudding
pŵer power
pwerau powers
pwerus powerful
pwll¹ pond, pool
pwll² coal-mine, pit
pwmp pump
pwnc subject, topic
pwrpas aim, object, purpose
pwrpasau purposes
pwrpasol purposeful
pwy who
Pwyl (Gwlad) Poland
pwyllgor committee
pwyllgorau committees
pwynt point, purpose
pwyntiau points
pwyntio to point
pwys¹ pound (weight)
pwys² emphasis, importance
pwys³ near
pwys⁴ nausea, near
pwysau¹ weights
pwysau² pressure, weight

pwysedd pressure
pwysicach more important
pwysicaf most important
pwysig important
pwysigrwydd importance, value
pwyslais emphasis, stress
pwysleisio to emphasise, to
  stress
pwysleisiodd (he/she/it)
  emphasised
pwyso to lean, to press, to weigh
pydru to putrefy, to rot
pyllau[1] pits
pyllau[2] pools

pymtheg fifteen
pymthegfed fifteenth
pynciau subjects
pynciol topical
pysgod fish(es)
pysgodfa fishery
pysgodfeydd fisheries
pysgodyn fish
pysgota to angle, to fish
pysgotwr angler, fisherman
pysgotwyr fishermen
pyst posts
pythefnos fortnight
pytiau snippets

R : r

a word starting with **r** printed in *italics* means that the root form
of that word begins with **rh**, e.g. *rad* root **rhad;**
or with **g**, e.g. *radd* root **gradd**

in a Welsh dictionary, unlike this list, **rh** is a letter in its own right and
follows *ry* and precedes *s* alphabetically

rad cheap
radd degree
raddau degrees
raddedig graduated
raddedigion graduates
raddfa scale
raddfeydd scales
raddio to graduate
raddol gradual
radiotherapi radiotherapy
ragfarn prejudice
Ragfyr December
raglen programme
raglenni programmes
ragnodir (is/will be) prescribed
ragor more
ragoriaeth excellence
ragorol excellent
ragweld to foresee
ragwelir (is/will be) foreseen
ragwelwyd (was) foreseen
rai some
raid must
rali rally
ramadeg grammar
ran part
ranbarth region

ranbarthau regions
ranbarthol regional
rannau parts
rannu to share
ras[1] race
ras[2] grace
rasio to race
rasys races
realaeth realism
realistig realistic
realiti reality
record record
recordiad recording
recordiadau recordings
recordiau records
recordio to record
recriwtio to recruit
red (he/she/it will) run
redeg to run
refeniw revenue
refferendwm referendum
reg curse
reidrwydd obligation
reilffordd railway
reilffyrdd railways
reis rice
reit quite

rendro to render
rennir (is/will be) divided, shared
rent rent
reol rule
reolaeth control
reolaidd regular
reolau rules
reoleiddio to regulate
reoli to rule
reoliad regulation
reoliadau regulations
reolir (is/will be) managed
reolwr manager
reolwyr managers
res row
restr list
restrir (is/will be) listed
restru to list
restrwyd (was) listed
reswm reason
resymau reasons
resymol reasonable
rew frost
rhad cheap, inexpensive
rhaeadr cascade, waterfall
rhaff rope, string
rhaffau ropes
rhag from, against, lest
rhagair foreword, preface
rhagarweiniad introduction
rhagarweiniol introductory,
   preliminary
rhagddi before her
rhagddo before him
rhagddynt before them
rhagdyb assumption,
   presupposition

rhagdybiaeth hypothesis,
   preconception
rhagdybiaethau preconceptions
rhagdybio to assume,
   to presuppose
rhagfarn bias, prejudice
rhagfynegi to foretell
Rhagfyr December
rhaglen program, programme
rhaglenni programmes
rhagnodi to prescribe
rhagnodir (is/will be) prescribed
rhagofalon precautions
rhagolwg outlook, prospect
rhagolygon prospects
rhagor more
rhagori to excel, to outdo,
   to surpass
rhagoriaeth distinction,
   excellence
rhagorol excellent, superb
rhagrith hypocrisy
rhagweithiol proactive
rhagweld to foresee
rhagwelir (is/will be) foreseen
rhagwelwyd (was) foreseen
rhagymadrodd introduction
rhai some
rhaid necessity
rhain these
rhamant romance
rhamantus romantic
rhan lot, part, portion, role, share
rhan-amser part-time
rhanbarth region
rhanbarthau regions
rhanbarthol divisional, regional

rhanddeiliad stakeholder
rhanddeiliaid stakeholders
rhaniad division, parting
rhaniadau divisions
rhannau parts
rhannol in part
rhannu to divide, to share,
    to distribute, to split
rhannwch (you) divide, share
rhannwyd (was) divided, shared
rhatach cheaper
rhed (he/she/it will) run
rhedeg to run, to flow,
    to conjugate
rhediad run, flow, slope
rhedodd (he/she/it) ran
rhedyn bracken, ferns
rheg curse, swear-word
rheidrwydd compulsion,
    necessity
rheilffordd railway
rheilffyrdd railways
rheini those
rheithgor jury
rhelyw remainder, the rest
rheng rank, row
rhennir (is/will be) divided,
    shared
rhent rent
rhenti rents
rhentu to rent
rheol rule
rheolaeth control, management
rheolaethau controls
rheolaethol managerial
rheolaidd regular
rheolau rules

rheoledig regulated
rheoleiddio to regulate
rheoli to control, to govern,
    to manage, to regulate, to rule
rheoliad regulation
rheoliadau regulations
rheoliadol regulatory
rheolir (is/will be) managed
rheolwr manager, ruler
rheolwraig manager (female)
rheolwyr managers
rheolydd regulator
rhes row, stripe, tier
rhesi rows
rhestr list, file, row
rhestrau lists
rhestredig listed
rhestri lists
rhestrir (is/will be) listed
rhestru to list
rhestrwch (you) list
rhestrwyd (was) listed
rheswm reason, explanation,
    cause
rhesymau reasons
rhesymedig reasoned
rhesymeg logic
rhesymegol logical
rhesymol reasonable
rhesymu to argue, to reason
rhew frost, ice
rhewi to freeze
rhiant parent
rhieni parents
rhif number
rhifau numbers
rhifedd numeracy

rhifo to count, to number
rhifyn issue, number
rhinwedd virtue
rhinweddau virtues
rhisgl bark, peel, rind
rhith guise, illusion, semblance
rhiw hill, slope
rho (you) give
rhodd¹ gift, present
rhodd² (he/she/it) gave
rhoddai (he/she/it would/ used to) give
rhoddi to give
rhoddion gifts
rhoddir (is/will be) given
rhoddodd (he/she/it) gave
rhoddwr giver
rhoddwyd (was) given
rhoddwyr givers
rhodfa promenade
rhodio to stroll, to walk
rhoes (he/she/it) gave
rhoi to give, to place, to put
rhoir (is/will be) given
rholio to roll
rhos heath, moor
rhostir heath
rhosyn rose
rhowch (you) give
Rhufain Rome
Rhufeinig Roman
rhugl fluent
rhuo to bellow, to roar
rhuthro to dash, to hurry, to rush
rhwng between
rhwyd net

rhwydd easy, fluent, free
rhwydi nets
rhwydwaith network
rhwydweithiau networks
rhwydweithio to network
rhwyg division, rift, split, tear
rhwygo to rip, to tear, to wrench
rhwym¹ bond, tie
rhwym² bound to, constipated
rhwymedigaeth obligation
rhwymedigaethau obligations
rhwymo to bind, to tie
rhwystr barrier, hindrance, obstruction
rhwystrau barriers
rhwystredigaeth frustration
rhwystro to block, to hinder, to prevent
rhy over, too
rhybudd caution, notice, warning
rhybuddio to caution, to warn
rhybuddion warnings
rhych furrow, rut, slot, trench
rhychwant span
rhyd ford
rhydd exempt, free, loose
rhyddfrydol liberal
rhyddha¹ (he/she/it) releases
rhyddha² (you) release!
rhyddhad liberation, relief
rhyddhau to free, to loosen, to release
rhyddhawyd (was) released
rhyddiaith prose
rhyddid freedom, liberty
rhyfedd odd, queer, strange, weird
rhyfeddod marvel, wonder

rhyfeddol amazing, marvellous, wonderful
rhyfeddu to amaze
rhyfel war
rhyfeloedd wars
rhyfelwr warrior
rhyfelwyr warriors
rhyngddo between him
rhyngddyn between them
rhyngddynt between them
rhyngoch between you
rhyngom between us
rhyngrwyd Internet
rhyngweithio to interact
rhyngweithiol interactive
rhyngwladol international
rhyngwyneb interface
rhythm rhythm
rhyw[1] some
rhyw[2] sex
rhywbeth something
rhywbryd sometime
rhywfaint a little, some, somewhat
rhywiol sexual, sexy
rhywioldeb sexuality
rhywle somewhere
rhywogaeth breed, species
rhywogaethau breeds, species
rhywrai some
rhywsut somehow
rhywun someone, somebody, person
riant parent
rieni parents
rif number
rifau numbers

rifo to count
rinwedd virtue
rinweddau virtues
risg risk
risgiau risks
risiau steps
ro gravel, shingle, earth
roc rock
roced rocket
rocedi rockets
rodd gift
roddai (he/she/it would/used to) give
roddi to give
roddion gifts
roddir (is/will be) given
roddodd (he/she/it) gave
roddwyd (was) given
roedd (he/she/it/there) was
roeddech (you) were
roeddem (we) were
roedden (they) were
roeddent (they) were
roeddwn (I) was
roeddynt (they) were
roes (he/she/it) gave
roi to give
roir (is/will be) given
rôl role
rolio to roll
rownd[1] round
rownd[2] around
rowndiau rounds
'run each, the one, the same
rŵan now
rwbel rubble
rwber eraser, rubber

Rwsia Russia
rwy (I) am
rwyd net
rwydd easy
rwydwaith network
rwydweithiau networks
rwyf[1] (I) am
rwyf[2] oar
rwymedigaeth obligation
rwymedigaethau obligations
rwymo to bind
rwystr barrier
rwystrau barriers
rwystro to hinder
rwyt (you) are
rybudd warning
rybuddio to warn
rydan (we) are
rydd free
ryddhad relief
ryddhau to free
ryddhawyd (was) released
ryddiaith prose
ryddid freedom

rydw (I) am
rydych (you) are
rydym (we) are
ryfedd strange
ryfeddod wonder
ryfeddol amazing
ryfel war
rygbi rugby
rym strength
rymus powerful
ryngwladol international
rysáit recipe
ryseitiau recipes
ryw[1] some
ryw[2] sex
rywbeth something
rywbryd sometime
rywfaint some
rywiol sexual
rywle somewhere
rywogaeth breed, species
rywogaethau species
rywsut somehow
rywun someone

S : s

Saboth Sabbath
sach sack
sachau sacks
Sadwrn[1] Saturday
Sadwrn[2] Saturn
saer carpenter, wright
Saesneg English (language)
Saeson English (people)
saeth arrow
saethau arrows
saethu to fire, to shoot
safai (he/she/it would/used to) stand
safbwynt standpoint, viewpoint
safbwyntiau points of view
saff safe
saffrwm crocus, saffron
safiad stand
safle location, position, site
safleoedd locations
safodd (he/she/it) stood
safon class, form, level, standard
safonau standards
safoni to standardise
safonol standard
safwe website
saib pause, rest
saif (he/she/it) stands
sail basis, foundation, ground
saim dripping, fat, grease
sain[1] sound, tone
sain[2] saint
saint saints

Sais Englishman
saith seven
saith deg seventy
saithdegau seventies
sâl[1] ill, poor, shoddy
sâl[2] sale
salad salad
salm psalm
salwch illness
sampl sample, specimen
samplau samples
samplo to sample
samplu to sample
sanau socks
sanctaidd hallowed, holy, sacred
sancteiddrwydd holiness, sanctity
sant saint
santes saint
sathru to trample, to tread
sawdl heel
sawl[1] many, several
sawl[2] however many, how many
saws sauce
Sbaen Spain
Sbaeneg Spanish (language)
sbardun accelerator, spur, throttle
sbarduno to spur, to spur (on)
sbectol glasses, spectacles
sbectrwm spectrum
sbel break, period, spell, time
sbesimen specimen

sbesimenau specimens
sbio to look
sbon brand new, spanking
sbort fun
sbri fun, hilarity
sbwriel refuse, rubbish, trash
sebon soap
sebra zebra
sector sector
sectorau sectors
sedd seat
seddau seats
seddi seats
sef namely, that is
sefydledig established
sefydliad establishment, institute, institution
sefydliadau institutions
sefydliadol institutional
sefydlir (is/will be) established
sefydlodd (he/she/it) established
sefydlog fixed, set, settled
sefydlogi to fix, to stabilise
sefydlogrwydd stability
sefydlu to establish, to install, to institute
sefydlwyd (was) established
sefyll to stand, to stay, to stop, to sit (an examination)
sefyllfa position, situation
sefyllfaoedd situations
segur idle, unemployed, unoccupied
seiat meeting
seibiant pause
seiciatrig psychiatric
seiciatryddol psychiatric

seiclo to bicycle, to cycle
seicoleg psychology
seicolegol psychological
seicolegwyr psychologists
seiliau foundations
seiliedig based
seilio to base
seilir (is/will be) based
seiliwyd (was) based
seiniau sounds
seintiau saints
Seisnig English
seithfed seventh
sêl seal, zeal
Seland Newydd New Zealand
selio to seal
selog ardent, zealous
semen semen
seminar seminar
seminarau seminars
senedd parliament, senate
seneddol parliamentary
sengl single
sensitif sensitive
sensitifrwydd sensitivity
sêr stars
serch[1] love
serch[2] although, despite, in spite
seremoni ceremony
seremonïau ceremonies
seren asterisk, star
sero nought, zero
serth precipitous, sheer, steep
sesiwn session
sesiynau sessions
set clique, set
setiau sets

setliad settlement
setlo to clear up, to settle
sewin sea-trout, sewin
sganio to scan
sgert skirt
sgi ski
sgidiau shoes
sgil following
sgìl skill
sgil-gynhyrchion by-products
sgiliau skills
sgio to ski
sglein polish, shine
sgleinio to glaze, to polish, to shine
sglodion chips
sgôr score
sgori to score
sgorio to score
sgoriodd (he/she/it) scored
sgrech scream, screech, shriek
sgrechain to scream, to shriek
sgrechian to screech
sgrifennu to write
sgrin screen, settle
sgriniau screens
sgrinio to screen
sgript script
sgriptiau scripts
sgriptio to script
sgwâr square, ring (boxing)
sgwennu to write
sgwrs chat, conversation, talk
sgwrsio to chat, to talk
sgyrsiau conversations
si buzz, hiss, rumour, whisper
siaced jacket

sialens challenge
sialensau challenges
siambr chamber
siambrau chambers
sianel channel
sianelau channels
sianeli channels
siani flewog caterpillar
siâp shape
Siapan Japan
siapiau shapes
siarad to speak, to talk
siaradwr speaker
siaradwyr speakers
siaredir (is/will be) spoken
Siarl Charles
siart chart
siarter charter
siartiau charts
siartr charter
siartredig chartered
siawns chance
sibrwd to whisper
sicr certain, sure
sicrhau to ensure, to assure, to fasten
sicrhawyd (was) ensured, assured
sicrhewch (you) ensure, assure
sicrwydd assurance, certainty, sureness
sidan silk
siec[1] cheque
siec[2] check
sieciau cheques
sied shed
sifil civil

sigaréts cigarettes
siglo to shake
silff ledge, shelf
silffoedd shelves
silindr cylinder
silio to spawn
sillaf syllable
sillafu to spell
silwair silage
simdde chimney
simne chimney
sin scene
sinc[1] zinc
sinc[2] sink
sinema cinema
sïo to murmur, to whiz
sioc shock
siocled chocolate
sioe show
sioeau shows
siom disappointment
siomedig disappointed,
   disappointing
siomi to disappoint
siop shop, workshop
siopa to shop
siopau shops
siopwr shopkeeper
sipsiwn gypsies
sir county, shire
siriol bright, cheerful, pleasant
siroedd counties
sirol county
si-so see-saw
siw nor sight nor sound
siwgr sugar
siwr certain, sure

siŵr sure
siwrnai[1] journey
siwrnai[2] once
siwt suit
sleid slide
sleidiau slides
slyri slurry
sment cement
smotyn pimple, speck, spot
smygu to smoke
sodiwm sodium
soffistigedig sophisticated
sofietaidd soviet
soia soya
solet solid
sôn[1] to mention, to talk
sôn[2] mention, sign, talk
soned sonnet
soniodd (he/she/it) mentioned
soniwyd (was) mentioned
sonnir (is/will be) mentioned
sos sauce
sosban saucepan
sosej sausage
soser saucer
sownd fast, sound, steady
stabl stable
stablau stables
stad estate, state
stadau estates
stadiwm stadium
stafell room
staff staff
staffio to staff
stamp stamp
stampiau stamps
statig static

statud statute
statudau statutes
statudol statutory
statws status
steddfod eisteddfod
steil[1] style
steil[2] surname
stêm steam
stiwdio studio
stoc stock
stociau stocks
stocio to stock
stôl chair, stool
stondin booth, stall
stondinau stalls
stop stop
stopio to stop
stôr fund, stock, store
storfa repository, store
storfeydd repositories
stori lie, story
storïau stories
storio to store
storm storm
stormydd storms
straen strain
straeon stories
strategaeth strategy
strategaethau strategies
strategol strategic
streic strike
stribed strip
stribedi strips
strôc seizure, stroke, stroke
   (of genius)
strwythur structure
strwythurau structures

strwythuredig structured
strwythuro to structure
strwythurol structural
stryd street
strydoedd streets
stumog stomach
stwff stuff
sudd juice, sap
suddo to sink, to pot, to putt
sugno to suck
Sul Sunday
sut how, what sort
sw zoo
swigod bubbles
swil bashful, demure, shy
Swistir Switzerland
switsh switch
switshis switches
swllt shilling
swm amount, sum
swmp bulk
swmpus bulky
sŵn noise, sound
swnio to sound
swnllyd noisy
swper supper
swydd[1] job, position, post
swydd[2] county
swyddfa office
swyddfeydd offices
swyddi jobs, posts
swyddog officer, official
swyddogaeth duty, function
swyddogaethau functions
swyddogaethol functional
swyddogion officers, officials
swyddogol official

swyn charm, spell, talisman
swyno to captivate, to charm,
    to enchant, to entrance
swynol captivating, charming
sy (who) is/are
sy'n (who) is/are
sych boring, dry, stale
sychder drought, dryness
syched thirst
sychu to dry, to wipe
sydd is/are
sydyn abrupt, sudden
syfrdanol astounding, stunning,
    stupendous
sylfaen base, basis, foundation
sylfaenol basic, fundamental,
    primary
sylfaenu to base, to found
sylfaenwr founder
sylfaenwyr founders
sylfaenydd founder
sylfeini foundations
syllu to gaze, to peer, to stare
sylw attention, comment,
    observation
sylwadau observations
sylwch (you) notice, observe
sylwedd essence, gist, substance
sylweddau substances
sylweddol significant, substantial
sylweddoli to realise
sylweddolodd (he/she/it) realised
sylwer (let it be) noticed,
    observed
sylwi to notice, to observe
sylwodd (he/she/it) noticed,
    observed

symbol symbol
symbolaidd symbolic
symbolau symbols
symbyliad encouragement,
    incentive, stimulus
symbylu to encourage,
    to stimulate
symiau sums
syml simple
symlach simpler
symleiddio to simplify
symptom symptom
symptomau symptoms
symud to budge, to move,
    to progress
symudedd mobility
symudiad motion, move,
    movement
symudiadau movements
symudodd (he/she/it) moved
symudol mobile, moveable
symudwyd (was) moved
syn amazed, astonished
synau sounds
syndod amazement, surprise,
    wonder
syndrom syndrome
synhwyrau senses
synhwyro to sense, to smell
synhwyrol rational, sensible
syniad concept, guess, idea,
    thought
syniadaeth conception
syniadau ideas
synnu to amaze, to astonish, to
    mystify, to surprise
synnwyr judgement, sense

syntheseiddio to synthesise
synthetig synthetic
syr sir
syrcas circus
syrfëwr surveyor
syrffio to surf

syrthio to fall
syrthiodd (he/she/it) fell
system system
systematig systematic
systemau systems
syth straight

T : t

a word starting with **th** printed in *italics* means that the root form
of that word begins with **rh**, e.g. *rad* root **rhad;**
or with **t**, e.g. *thad* root **tad**

in a Welsh dictionary, unlike this list, **th** is a letter in its own right and
follows *ry* and precedes *s* alphabetically

tabernacl tabernacle
tabl table
tablau tables
tabled tablet
tabledi tablets
Tachwedd November
tacsi taxi
tad father
tadau fathers
tad-cu grandfather
tadolaeth fatherhood, paternity
taenu to spread
Taf Taff (river)
tafarn inn, pub, public house,
   tavern
tafarnau pubs
tafarndai inns
tafarndy inn, public house
taflen leaflet
taflenni leaflets
taflodd (he/she/it) threw
taflu to cast, to discard, to throw
tafod element, spit, tongue
tafodiaith dialect
Tafwys Thames
tagfa blockage, choking, jam
tagfeydd jams

tai houses
taid grandfather
tail dung, manure
tair three
taith journey
tal tall
tâl fee, payment
talcen forehead
taleb receipt, voucher
talebau vouchers
talent talent
talentog talented
taliad payment
taliadau payments
talm period
talu to pay
talwm while
talwrn arena, competition
talwyd (was) paid
tamaid bit, morsel, snippet
tan¹ under
tan² until
tân fire
tanat under you
tanau fires
tanbaid fiery, incandescent
tanc tank

tanciau tanks
tanddaearol subterranean, underground
tangnefedd peace
tanio to fire, to ignite, to start
tanlinellu to underline
tanllyd fiery
tano under him
tanau strings
tanseilio to subvert, to undermine
tanwydd fuel
tanysgrifio to subscribe
tap tap
tâp tape
tapiau taps
tarddiad derivation, source
tarddu to derive from, to originate
tarfu to disturb, to interrupt, to scare
targed butt, target
targedau targets
targedu to target
taro to hit, to strike, to suit
tarw bull
tasg task
tasgau tasks
tasglu task force
tatws potatoes
taw[1] silence
taw[2] (you) be quiet!
taw[3] that it is, that it was
tawel calm, muted, quiet, silent, still
tawelu to calm, to placate, to quieten
tawelwch calm, quiet, stillness

te tea
tebot teapot
tebyg[1] like, similar, likely
tebyg[2] likelihood
tebygol likely, probable
tebygolrwydd likelihood, probability
tebygrwydd likeness, resemblance, similarity
tecell kettle
techneg technique
technegau techniques
technegol technical
technoleg technology
technolegau technologies
technolegol technological
teclyn thingamajig, tool
teg fair, fairly, fine
tegan toy
teganau toys
tegell kettle
tegwch beauty, fairness
teiar tyre
teiars tyres
teilwng deserving, worthy
teilyngdod merit, worthiness
teimlad feeling, sentiment
teimladau sentiments
teimlai (he/she/it would/ used to) feel
teimlo to feel
teimlwn[1] (we/we will) feel
teimlwn[2] (I would/used to) feel
teip print, type
teipio to type
teirgwaith three times, thrice
teisen cake

teithiau journeys
teithio to travel
teithiol peripatetic, travelling
teithiwr passenger, traveller
teithwyr passengers, travellers
teitl title
teitlau titles
telathrebu to telecommunicate
teledu television, television set
teleffon telephone
telerau terms
telir (is/will be) paid
telyn harp
telyneg lyric
teml temple
temtasiwn temptation
tenant tenant
tenantiaeth tenancy
tenantiaid tenants
tenau slim, sparse, thin, threadbare
tendr tender
tendro to tender
tensiwn tension
teras terrace
terfyn boundary, end, limit
terfynau bounds
terfynol final
terfynu to end, to terminate
term term
termau terms
testament testament
testun subject, text
testunau subjects
testunol textual, topical
teulu family, household
teuluaidd ancestral, domestic, familial

teuluoedd families
teuluol ancestral, domestic, familial
tew fat, thick
teyrnas kingdom
teyrnasiad reign
teyrnasu to reign, to rule
teyrngarwch allegiance, loyalty
teyrnged tribute
TGAU GCSE
thad father
thad-cu grandfather
thaflenni pamphlets
thaflu to throw
thai houses
thair three
thaith journey
thâl payment
thaliadau payments
thalu to pay
than[1] until
than[2] under
thân fire
tharged target
thargedau targets
thargedu to target
tharo to strike
thasgau tasks
the tea
theatr theatre
thebyg similar
thechnegau techniques
thechnegol technical
thechnoleg technology
theg fair
theimladau feelings
theimlo to feel

theirgwaith three times
theithiau journeys
theithio to travel
theitl title
theledu television
thelerau terms
thema theme
thematig thematic
themâu themes
thenantiaid tenants
theori theory
therapi therapy
therapiwtig therapeutic
therapydd therapist
therapyddion therapists
thestun subject, text
thestunau subjects, texts
theulu family
theuluoedd families
thi you
thîm team
thimau teams
thipyn bit
thir land
thirfeddianwyr landowners
thlodi poverty
thorri to break
thra[1] very
thra[2] while
thraddodiadau traditions
thraean one third
thraed feet
thrafnidiaeth traffic
thrafod to discuss
thrafodaeth discussion
thrafodaethau discussions
thrais rape, violence

thramor abroad
thraw there
thref town
threfi towns
threfn order
threfniadau arrangements
threfnu to arrange
threftadaeth heritage
threuliau expenses
thri three
thrigain sixty
thrigolion inhabitants
thrin to treat
thriniaeth treatment
thro[1] turn, bend
thro[2] journey
thro[3] time
throi to turn, to twist, to stir,
     to dig, to upset, to change
thros over
throseddau crimes, offences
throseddwyr criminals
throsglwyddo to transfer
throsodd for, over
thrwsio to repair
thrwy through
thrwyn nose
thrydan electricity
thu side
thua about
thwf growth
thwristiaeth tourism
thwyll deceit
thyfu to grow
thymor term
thynnu to draw
thystiolaeth evidence

ti you
tic tick
ticio to tick
ticiwch (you) tick
tîm team
timau teams
tin anus, bum
tincar tinker
tipyn little, (quite) a bit
tir ground, land
tirfeddiannwr landowner
tirfeddianwyr landowners
tiriogaeth dominion, territory
tiriogaethol territorial
tirion gentle
tirlenwi to landfill
tirlun landscape
tirlunio to landscape
tiroedd lands
tirwedd landscape, relief
tirweddau landscapes
tisian to sneeze
tithau yourself
tiwb tube
tiwtor tutor
tiwtoriaid tutor
tlawd impoverished, poor
tlodi¹ impoverishment, poverty
tlodi² to make poor
tlodion poor (people)
tlos pretty
tlotaf poorest
tlws¹ award, gem, jewel, trophy
tlws² pretty
to¹ roof
to² generation
toc¹ soon

toc² piece, slice
tocyn¹ tag, ticket, token
tocyn² slice, packed lunch
tocynnau tickets
toddi to blend, to dissolve,
    to melt, to thaw
toddydd solvent
toddyddion solvents
toiled toilet
toiledau toilets
toll custom, duty, levy, tariff, toll
tollau tariffs
tom dung, manure
tomato tomato
tomatos tomatoes
tomen dump, dunghill, mound
ton billow, wave
tôn¹ tune
tôn² tone
tonau tunes, tones
tonnau waves
top top
tor¹ belly, litter, underside
tor² break
torf crowd
torfol collective, mass
Tori Tory
toriad break, cutting, fracture
toriadau cuttings
Torïaid Tories
torri to break, to cut, to fell,
    to mow, to sever
torrodd (he/she/it) broke, cut
tost¹ toast
tost² ill, sore, unwell
tra¹ extremely, very
tra² while, whilst**

trac track
trachefn again
tractor tractor
traddodi to commit, to deliver
traddodiad tradition
traddodiadau traditions
traddodiadol traditional
traean one third
traed feet
traeth beach, sands
traethau beaches
traethawd composition, dissertation, essay
traethlin shoreline
traethodau dissertations, essays
trafferth bother, trouble
trafferthion difficulties
traffig traffic
trafnidiaeth traffic
trafod to discuss, to handle, to negotiate
trafodaeth discussion, negotiation
trafodaethau discussions
trafodion proceedings, transactions
trafodir (is/will be) discussed
trafodwch (you) discuss
trafodwyd (was) discussed
tragwyddol eternal
tragywydd for ever
trahaus arrogant, haughty
trais force, rape, violence
Trallwng Welshpool
tramgwydd hindrance, offence
tramgwyddau hindrances
tramor foreign, overseas

tramwyo to traverse
trannoeth the next day
tras kin, lineage, pedigree
traul consumption, expense, wear
traw pitch (sound)
trawiad blow, stroke
trawiadol striking
traws cross
trawsnewid to convert, to transform
tre town
trech stronger, superior
trechu to defeat, to overpower
tref home, town
Trefaldwyn Montgomery
trefi towns
trefn order, procedure
trefniad arrangement
trefniadaeth organisation, procedure
trefniadau arrangements
trefniadol procedural
trefniant arrangement
trefnir (is/will be) arranged, organised
trefnu to arrange, to organise
trefnus methodical, orderly
trefnwyd (was) arranged, organised
trefnwyr organisers
trefnydd organiser
trefol urban
treftadaeth heritage, inheritance
treial trial
treialon trials
treiddio to penetrate, to pervade

treigl motion, passage
treiglo[1] to mutate
treiglo[2] to roll, to trickle, to trundle
treisgar violent
treisiol violent
trên engine, train
trenau trains
treth rate, tax
trethadwy taxable
trethi taxes
trethiannol rateable
trethu to tax, to rate
treuliau expenses
treulio to spend, to digest, to wear
treuliodd (he/she/it) spent
tri three
tribiwnlys tribunal
tribiwnlysoedd tribunals
tridegau thirties
trigain sixty
trigo to die, to dwell
trigolion inhabitants
trin to cultivate, to handle, to treat
trindod trinity, Trinity
triniaeth treatment
triniaethau treatments
trio to try
triongl triangle
trip trip
trist sad, tragic
tristwch sadness, sorrow
tro[1] turn, bend, change
tro[2] journey, walk
tro[3] time
tro[4] (you) turn!

trochi to dip, to dirty, to immerse
trodd (he/she/it) turned
troed foot, base
troedfedd foot (length)
troedfeddi feet (distance)
troellog twisting, winding
troeon[1] turns, bends, changes
troeon[2] times
troi to turn, to stir, to twist, to dig, to upset, to change
trol cart
trom heavy
tros for, over
trosedd crime, offence
troseddau offences
troseddol criminal
troseddu to commit an offence, to transgress
troseddwr criminal, culprit
troseddwyr criminals, culprits
trosglwyddiad conveyance, transference
trosglwyddiadau conveyances
trosglwyddir (is/will be) transferred
trosglwyddo to convey, to transfer, to transmit, to transport
trosglwyddwyd (was) transferred
trosi to convert, to translate, to turn
trosiannol transitional
trosiant conversion, turnover
trosodd over
trosolwg overview

trosom for us, over us
trosti for her, over her
trosto for him, over him
trostynt for them, over them
trothwy doorstep, threshold
trowch (you) turn
trowyd (was) turned
truan[1] poor fellow, wretch
truan[2] poor, wretched
trueni[1] pity
trueni[2] what a pity!
truenus pitiful, wretched
trugaredd compassion, mercy
trugarog compassionate, merciful
trwch coating, layer, thickness
trwchus thick
trwm heavy, sad
trwodd through
trwot through you
trwsio to mend, to smarten
trwy by means of, through, because, as
trwyadl exhaustive, thorough
trwydded licence, permit
trwyddedau licences
trwyddedig licensed, qualified
trwyddedu to license
trwyddi through her/it
trwyddo through him/it
trwyddynt through them
trwyn nose, nozzle, promontory
trychineb catastrophe, disaster
trydan electric current, electricity
trydanol electric, electrical
trydedd third

trydydd third
tryloyw translucent, transparent
trylwyr thorough
trymion heavy
trysor treasure
trysorau treasures
Trysorlys Treasury
trysorydd treasurer
trywydd track, trail
tu side
tua about, c., circa, towards
tuag about, towards
tudalen page
tudalennau pages
Tuduriaid Tudors
tuedd tendency, propensity, bias
tueddiad tendency
tueddiadau tendencies
tueddol inclined, liable, susceptible
tueddu to tend to
tun tin
tunnell ton
turio to burrow, to drill
twbercwlosis tuberculosis
twf growth
twll burrow, hole, puncture
twnnel tunnel
twp daft, obtuse, stupid
twr crowd, heap, tor
twr̂ tower
twrci turkey
Twrci Turkey
twristaidd tourist
twristiaeth tourism
twristiaid tourists
twrnai attorney, lawyer

twt[1] dapper, neat, tidy
twt[2] rubbish!, tut!
twyll deceit, fraud
twyllo to cheat, to deceive, to fool
twym hot, warm
twyn dune, hillock, knoll, sand-dune
twyni dunes
tŷ house
tyb opinion, surmise
tybaco tobacco
tybed I wonder
tybiaeth presumption
tybiedig putative, supposed
tybio to suppose, to assume, to presume
tybir (is/will be) assumed
Tyddewi St. Davids
tyddyn croft, dwelling, smallholding
tydi[1] it is you, you yourself
tydi[2] (he/she/it) is not
tyfiant growth, tumour, vegetation
tyfodd (he/she/it) grew
tyfu to grow, to increase
tyllau holes
tyllu to bore, to burrow, to excavate
tylwyth family, kindred
tymheredd temperature
tymhorau seasons, terms
tymhorol seasonable, seasonal, temporal
tymor season, term
tyndra strain, tension, tightness

tyner delicate, gentle, mild, tender
tynged destiny, fate
tyngedfennol fateful
tyniad pull, subtraction
tyniadau attractions
tynnir[1] (is/will be) pulled, subtracted, removed
tynnir[2] (is/will be) drawn, photographed
tynnodd[1] (he/she/it) pulled, subtracted, removed
tynnodd[2] (he/she/it) drew, photographed
tynnu[1] to pull, to subtract, to remove
tynnu[2] to draw, to photograph
tynnwch[1] (you) pull, subtract, remove
tynnwch[2] (you) draw, photograph
tynnwyd[1] (was) pulled, subtracted, removed
tynnwyd[2] (was) drawn, photographed
tyrd (you) come!
tyrfa crowd, multitude
tyst witness
tystio to testify, to witness
tystiolaeth evidence, testimony
tystion witnesses
tystysgrif certificate, diploma
tystysgrifau certificates
tywallt to pour
tywod sand
tywydd weather
tywyll black, blind, dark, obscure

tywyllwch dark, darkness, night
tywys to guide, to lead
tywysog prince

tywysoges princess
tywysogion princes

U : u

uchaf topmost, uppermost
uchafbwynt climax, pinnacle
uchafbwyntiau highlights
uchafswm maximum
uchder altitude, height
uchel high, loud
ucheldir highland, upland
ucheldiroedd highlands
uchelgais ambition
uchelgeisiol ambitious
uchelwr nobleman
uchelwyr noblemen
uchod above
UDA USA
uffern hell
ufudd dutiful, obedient
ufuddhau to obey
ugain twenty
ugeinfed twentieth
ugeiniau twenties
un[1] one
un[2] one, same, very
un[3] each, one
unai (he/she/it would) unite
undeb union, unity
undebau unions
undod unity
undydd day, one-day
uned unit
unedau units
unedig united
unedol unitary
unfed first

unffurf uniform
unfryd unanimous
unfrydol unanimous
uniaethu to identify with
uniaith monoglot
unig lone, lonely, only, sole
unigol individual, singular
unigolion individuals
unigolyn individual
unigrwydd loneliness
unigryw unique
union direct, erect, exact, precise, straight, upright
uniongyrchol direct
unioni to justify, to rectify, to straighten
unionsyth point-blank, upright, vertical
unllawr one-storey
unlle anywhere, same place
unman anywhere
uno to amalgamate, to join, to unite
unol united
unrhyw any, any (old)
unrhyw beth anything
unrhyw un anyone
unwaith once
urdd guild, order
urddas dignity, nobility
urddasol dignified, noble, stately
ustus magistrate
uwch advanced, higher, senior

uwchben above, over, overhead
uwchefrydiau advanced studies
uwchgynghrair premiership,
   super-league

uwchlaw above
uwchradd secondary
uwchraddio to upgrade

W : w

a word starting with **w** printed in *italics* means that the root form
of that word begins with **g**, e.g. *waed* root **gwaed**

waed blood
wael ill, poor
waelod bottom
waered down
waeth worse
waethaf worst
wag empty
wahân apart
wahaniaeth difference
wahaniaethau differences
wahaniaethu to differ,
    to discriminate, to distinguish
wahanol different
wahanu to part
wahardd to forbid
wahodd to invite
wahoddiad invitation
waith work
wal wall
wal dân firewall
waliau walls
wallau mistakes
wallt hair
wan weak
war scruff
warant guarantee
warantu to guarantee
warchod to baby-sit, to guard
warchodaeth conservation
ward ward
wardiau wards

waredu to dispose of
wariant expenditure
wario to spend
wariwyd (was) spent
wartheg cattle
was farm-hand, lad
wasanaeth service
wasanaethau services
wasanaethir (is/will be)
    served
wasanaethu to serve
wasg press
wasgar scattered
wasgnodau imprints
wasgu to press
wastad constant, flat
wastraff wastage
wastraffu to waste
wawr dawn
wddf neck, throat
we web
wedd appearance
weddi prayer
weddill remainder
weddillion remnants
weddïo to pray
weddol fair
weddw widow
wedi[1] (that) has/have
    wedi'i[1] (that) has/have {...}
    him/her/it

wedi'u¹ (that) has/have {...} them
wedi² after
  wedi'i² after his/her/its
  wedi'u² after their
wedyn afterwards, next, then
wefan website
wefannau websites
wefr charge, shock, thrill
wefus lip
weiddi to shout
weini to serve
weinidog minister
weinidogaeth ministry
weinidogion ministers
weinyddiaeth ministry
weinyddir (is/will be) administered
weinyddol administrative
weinyddu to serve
weision servants
weithdai workshops
weithdrefn procedure
weithdrefnau procedures
weithfeydd works
weithgar diligent
weithgaredd activity
weithgareddau activities
weithgarwch diligence
weithiau occasionally, sometimes
weithio to work
weithiodd (he/she/it) worked
weithiwr worker
weithlu workforce
weithred action
weithrediad operation
weithrediadau actions
weithredir (is/will be) done

weithredoedd deeds
weithredol acting
weithredu to act
weithredwr operator
weithredwyr operators
weithwyr workers
wel well!
wêl (he/she/it) sees, behold!
weladwy visible
welaf (I/I will) see
welai (he/she/it would/used to) see
welais (I) saw
weld to see
wele behold!
weled to see
weledigaeth vision
weledol visual
welir (is/will be) seen
well better
wella to improve
welliannau improvements
welliant improvement
wellt straw
welodd (he/she/it) saw
welsant (they) saw
welsoch (you) saw
welsom (we) saw
welwch (you) see
welwn (we/we will) see
welwyd (was) seen
wely bed
welyau beds
wen¹ white
wen² goitre
wên smile
wendid weakness

wendidau weaknesses
Wener[1] Friday
Wener[2] Venus
wennol swallow
wenu to smile
wenwyn poison
wenwynig poisonous
werdd green
werin folk
weriniaeth republic
wers lesson
wersi lessons
wersyll camp
werth value
werthfawr valuable
werthfawrogi to appreciate
werthiant sales
werthir (is/will be) sold
werthodd (he/she/it) sold
werthoedd values
werthu to sell
werthuso to evaluate
werthwyd (was) sold
westai guest
westy guest house
wiced stump, wicket
wifren wire
win wine
wir truth
wireddu to realise
wirfoddol voluntary
wirfoddolwyr volunteers
wirio to check
wirion silly
wirionedd truth
wironeddol truly
wisg clothing

wisgo to dress
wiw[1] fine
wiw[2] dare not
wiwer squirrel
wlad country
wladfa colony, Patagonia
wladwriaeth state
wladwriaethau states
wlân wool
wledd feast
wledig rural
wledydd countries
wleidyddiaeth politics
wleidyddion politicians
wleidyddol political
wlyb wet
wn[1] gun
wn[2] (I) know
wna[1] (he/she/it) does, makes
wna[2] (you) do!, make!
wnaed (was) done, made
wnaeth (he/she/it) did, made
wnaethant (they) did, made
wnaethoch (you) did, made
wnaethom (we) did, made
wnaethon (they) did, made
wnaethpwyd (was) done, made
wnaf (I/I will) do, make
wnaiff (he/she/it will) do, make
wnânt (they/they will) do, make
wnawn (we/we will) do, make
wnei (you/you will) do, make
wneid (would be/used to be) done, made
wneir (is/will be) done, made
wnelo (he/she/it were to) do, make

wnes (I) did, made
wneud to do, to make
wneuthur to do, to make
wneuthurwyr makers, manufacturers
wnewch (you/you will) do, make
wobr prize
wobrau prizes
wobrwyo to award
wragedd ladies, wives
wraidd root
wraig wife, woman
wrandawiad hearing
wrando to hear
Wranws Uranus
wreiddiau roots
wreiddiol original
wres heat
wrth because, by, from, towards, (up) to, while
wrthdaro to clash, to collide
wrthi at it, from her, to her
wrtho at it, from him, to him
wrthod to refuse
wrthrych object
wrthrychau objects
wrthrychol objective
wrthsefyll to withstand
wrthwynebiad objection
wrthwynebu to object to
wrthych from you, to you
wrthyf from me
wrthym from us, to us
wrthyn from them, to them
wrthynt from them, to them
wrthyt from you, to you
wthio to push

wy[1] egg
wy[2] (I) am
wyau eggs
wybod to know
wybodaeth information, knowledge
wybyddus known
wych superb
ŵydd goose
wyddai (he/she/it would/used to) know
Wyddfa Snowdon
Wyddgrug Mold
wyddoch (you) know
wyddom (we) know
wyddoniaeth science
wyddonol scientific
wyddor alphabet, rudiments
wyddost (you) know
wyddwn (I would/used to) know
wyddys (it is) known
wydr glass
wyf (I) am
wyliadwrus alert
wyliau holidays
wylio to beware, to keep watch, to look out, to observe, to take care of, to tend, to watch
wyllt wild
wylo to weep
wylo to cry, to weep
wylwyr viewers
wyn white
ŵyn lambs
wyna to lamb
wyneb facade, face, surface
wynebau faces

wynebu to face
wynt wind
ŵyr[1] grandson
ŵyr[2] (he/she/it) knows
ŵyr[3] crooked, slanting
wyrdd green, unripe
wyrth miracle
wysg track, wake

wyt (you) are
wyth eight
wythdegau eighties
wythfed[1] eighth
wythfed[2] octave
wythnos week
wythnosau weeks
wythnosol weekly

Y : y

a word starting with **y** printed in *italics* means that the root form
of that word begins with **g**, e.g. *yrru* root **gyrru**

y¹ the, per
y² that
    y'ch that {...} you
    y'i that {...} him/her/it
    y'm that {...} me
    y'u that {...} them
ych ox
ychwaith either
ychwaneg extra
ychwanegiad addition,
   supplement
ychwanegiadau additions
ychwanegion extras
ychwanegir (is/will be) added
ychwanegodd (he/she/it)
   added
ychwanegol additional, extra
ychwanegu to add, to augment,
   to supplement
ychwanegwch (you) add
ychwanegwyd (was) added
ychydig few, little
ŷd corn
ydach (you) are
ydan (we) are
ydi (he/she/it) is, is (he/she/it)?
ydoedd (he/she/it) was
ydw (I) am, am (I)?
ydwyf (I) am, am (I)?
ydwyt (you) are, are (you)?

ydy (he/she/it) is/are, is/are
   (he/she/it)?
ydych (you) are, are (you)?
ydym (we) are, are (we)?
ydyn (they) are, are (they)?
ydynt (they) are, are (they)?
ydyw (he/she/it) is, is (he/she/it)?
yfed to drink, to imbibe,
   to tipple
yfory tomorrow
ym in
yma here, present, this
ymadael to leave, to part
ymadawedig deceased
ymadawiad departure, parting
ymaddasu to acclimatise,
   to adapt
ymadrodd expression, phrase
ymadroddion expressions
ymaelodi to become a member,
   to join
ymagwedd attitude
ymagweddau attitudes
ymaith away, hence, off
ymarfer¹ to exercise, to practise,
   to rehearse, to train
ymarfer² rehearsal, practice,
   exercise
ymarferiad practice, exercise
ymarferion exercises

ymarferol practical, realistic, workable
ymarferoldeb practicality
ymarferwr practitioner
ymarferwyr practitioners
ymarferydd practitioner
ymatal to abstain, to refrain
ymateb[1] to respond
ymateb[2] reaction, response
ymatebion responses
ymatebodd (he/she/it) responded
ymatebol responding
ymatebwr respondent
ymatebwyr respondents
ymatebydd respondent
ymbelydredd radioactivity
ymbelydrol radioactive
ymborth food, sustenance
ymchwil research
ymchwiliad inquiry, investigation
ymchwiliadau inquiries
ymchwilio to explore, to investigate
ymchwiliol investigative, research
ymchwiliwr explorer, investigator, researcher
ymchwilwyr investigators
ymchwilydd investigator
ymddangos to appear, to seem
ymddangosai (he/she/it would/used to) appear
ymddangosiad appearance
ymddangosiadol apparent, seeming
ymddangosodd (he/she/it) appeared

ymddengys (he/she/it) appears
ymddeol to retire
ymddeoliad retirement
ymddiddori to take an interest in
ymddiheuriad apology
ymddiheuriadau apologies
ymddiheuro to apologise
ymddiried to trust
ymddiriedaeth confidence, trust
ymddiriedolaeth trust
ymddiriedolaethau trusts
ymddiriedolwr trustee
ymddiriedolwyr trustees
ymddiswyddiad resignation
ymddiswyddo to resign
ymddwyn to behave
ymddygiad behaviour, conduct, manners
ymdeimlad feeling
ymdoddi to blend, to fuse, to melt
ymdopi to cope, to manage
ymdrech attempt, effort, exertion
ymdrechion efforts
ymdrechu to endeavour, to strive
ymdrin to deal, to treat
ymdriniaeth treatment
ymdriniwyd (was) treated
ymdrinnir (is/will be) treated
ymdrochi to bathe
ymelwa to exploit
ymennydd brain
ymerodraeth empire
ymestyn to extend, to reach, to stretch

ymestynnol challenging, extending

ymfalchïo to pride oneself, to take pride in

ymfudo to emigrate

ymgais attempt, effort, endeavour

ymgartrefu to settle in

ymgasglu to congregate

ymgeisio to apply, to try

ymgeiswyr applicants

ymgeisydd applicant, candidate, competitor

ymgorffori to embody, to enshrine

ymgyfarwyddo to familiarise oneself

ymgymeriad undertaking

ymgymerwr undertaker

ymgymerwyd (was) undertaken

ymgymerwyr undertakers

ymgymryd to undertake

ymgynghori to confer, to consult

ymgynghoriad consultation

ymgynghorir (is/will be) consulted

ymgynghorol advisory, consultative

ymgynghorwyd (was) consulted

ymgynghorwyr advisers, consultants

ymgynghorydd adviser, consultant

ymgyngoriadau consultations

ymgynnull to assemble, to gather

ymgyrch campaign, drive, expedition

ymgyrchoedd campaigns

ymgyrchu to campaign

ymgyrchwr campaigner

ymgyrchwyr campaigners

ymgyrraedd to strive for

ymhel to be concerned, to meddle, to tamper

ymhél to be concerned, to meddle, to tamper

ymhelaethiad elaboration

ymhelaethu to elaborate, to expand upon

ymhell afar, far

ymhellach further

ymhen by, in

ymhle where

ymhlith amongst

ymhlyg implicit, intrinsic

ymhob in every

ymholi to inquire

ymholiad enquiry, inquiry

ymholiadau inquiries

ymhyfrydu to delight in, to revel

ymlacio to relax

ymladd to combat, to compete, to fight

ymlaen ahead, on, onward

ymlediad aneurism, diffusion, dilation, expansion

ymledol spreading

ymledu to dilate, to spread, to suffuse

ymlusgiad reptile

ymlusgiaid reptiles

ymlyniad adherence, attachment

ymofyn to fetch, to get, to seek, to want

ymolchi to wash, to wash (oneself)

ymorol to seek, to take care

ymosod to assail, to assault, to attack

ymosodiad assault, attack, onslaught

ymosodiadau attacks

ymosododd (he/she/it) attacked

ymosodol aggressive, attacking

ymosodwr attacker

ymroddedig devoted

ymroddiad devotion

ymroi to devote

ymron almost

ymrwymedig committed

ymrwymiad commitment, undertaking

ymrwymiadau commitments

ymrwymo to commit oneself

ymryson[1] contest, rivalry

ymryson[2] to compete, to contend, to contest

ymsefydlu to establish, to establish oneself

ymson[1] monologue, soliloquy

ymson[2] to soliloquise

ymuno to join, to join in

ymunodd (he/she/it) joined

ymunwch (you) join

ymunwyd (was) joined

ymwadiad renunciation

ymwadiadau denials

ymweld to call, to visit

ymweliad call, visit

ymweliadau visits

ymwelodd (he/she/it) visited

ymwelwch (you) visit

ymwelwr caller, visitor

ymwelwyd (was) visited

ymwelwyr visitors

ymwelydd visitor

ymwneud to concern, to do with, to pertain to

ymwrthod to abstain

ymwthiol intrusive

ymwybod consciousness

ymwybodol aware, conscious

ymwybyddiaeth awareness, consciousness

ymyl border, edge, side, verge

ymylol marginal

ymylon fringes

ymyriad intervention

ymyriadau interventions

ymyrraeth interference, intervention, meddling

ymyrryd to intervene, to intrude, to meddle

ymysg among, amongst, between

yn[1] at, in, to

yn[2] is/are, was/were, will be

yna then, there, whereupon

ynad justice, magistrate

ynadon magistrates

ynddi in her/it

ynddo in him/it

ynddyn in them

ynddynt in them

yng in

yngan to pronounce, to speak, to utter

ynganu to enunciate
ynghanol in the middle of
ynghlwm tied up
ynghyd together
ynghylch about, concerning
ynghynt quicker, sooner
ynglŷn with regard
ynni energy
yno there
ynof in me
ynom in us
ynot in you
yntau himself
yntê isn't it?
ynteu or, then, therefore
ynys island, isle
ynysig insular, isolated
ynysoedd islands
ynysu to insulate, to isolate,
    to maroon
yr the
yrfa career
yrfaoedd careers
yrru to drive
yrrwr driver
yrwyr drivers
ys as
ysbaid respite, spell
ysbeidiol intermittent,
    spasmodic, sporadic
ysblander splendour
ysblennydd resplendent, splendid
ysbryd ghost, mettle, morale,
    spirit
ysbrydion ghosts
ysbrydol religious, spiritual
ysbrydoledig inspired

ysbrydoli to inspire
ysbrydoliaeth inspiration
ysbwriel rubbish
ysbytai hospitals
ysbyty hospice, hospital, infirmary
ysfa craving, itch
ysgafn gentle, light, slight
ysgafnach lighter
ysgariad divorce
ysgaru to divorce, to separate
ysglyfaeth prey, victim
ysgogi to impel, to move, to stir
ysgogiad impulse
ysgogol stimulating
ysgol[1] ladder
ysgol[2] school
ysgolhaig intellectual, scholar
ysgolheictod learning,
    scholarship
ysgolheigaidd scholarly
ysgolheigion intellectuals
ysgolion schools
ysgoloriaeth scholarship
ysgoloriaethau scholarships
ysgrif essay
ysgrifau essays
ysgrifen handwriting, writing
ysgrifenedig written
ysgrifennodd (he/she/it) wrote
ysgrifennu to write
ysgrifennwch (you) write
ysgrifennwr writer
ysgrifennwyd (was) written
ysgrifennydd secretary
ysgrifenwyr writers
ysgrifenyddiaeth secretaryship
ysgrifenyddion secretaries

ysgrifenyddol secretarial
ysgrythur scripture
ysgubol sweeping
ysgubor barn, granary
ysgwyd to flap, to shake, to wag
ysgwydd shoulder
ysgwyddau shoulders
ysgwyddo to shoulder
ysgyfaint lungs
ysgytwol jolting, shocking
ysmygu to smoke
ystad estate, state
ystâd estate
ystadau estates
ystadegau statistics
ystadegol statistical
ystafell room
ystafelloedd rooms
ystatud statute
ystlum bat (creature)
ystlumod bats (creatures)
ystlys flank, side, touchline
ystod¹ during
ystod² range

ystum bend, curve, pose, posture, stance
ystyr meaning, sense
ystyriaeth consideration, factor
ystyriaethau considerations
ystyrid (would be/used to be) considered
ystyried to consider, to ponder
ystyriodd (he/she/it) considered
ystyriol considerate, thoughtful
ystyrir (is/will be) considered
ystyriwch (you) consider
ystyriwyd (was) considered
ystyrlon meaningful
ystyron meanings
ysu to consume, to crave, to itch, to yearn
ysw. Esq.
yswiriant insurance
yswiriwr insurer
yswaeth alas, unfortunately
yw¹ is/are
  yw'ch is/are your
  yw'r is/are the
yw² yews

12/14